AND WHAT WAS I DOING THERE?

Stories from the 174th Ordnance Detachment in Vietnam

WILLIAM B. McCORMICK

HELLGATE PRESS   ASHLAND, OREGON

And What Was I Doing There?

Published by Hellgate Press

(An imprint of L&R Publishing, LLC)

Hellgate Press
PO Box 3531
Ashland, OR 97520
www.hellgatepress.com

Editing: Harley B. Patrick
Cover design: L. Redding

Library of Congress Cataloging-in-Publication Data

McCormick, William B.

  And what was I doing there? : stories from the 174th Ordnance Detachment in Vietnam
/ William B. McCormick. -- First edition.

    pages cm

ISBN 978-1-55571-723-0

1. McCormick, William B. 2. Vietnam War, 1961-1975--Personal narratives, Ameri-
can. 3. United States. Army. Ordnance Detachment, 174th. 4. Soldiers--United States-
-Biography. 5. United States. Army--Military life--History--20th century. 6. United
States. Army--Ordnance and ordnance stores--History--20th century. I. Title.

DS558.4.M38 2012

959.704'34--dc23

                    2012039486

Printed and bound in the United States of America
First edition 10 9 8 7 6 5 4 3 2

*To Sergeant John E. Nelson, C Company, 2nd Battalion,
22nd Infantry, 25th Division. Killed in Action, April 13, 1968.
Friends forever.*

CONTENTS

Preface and Acknowledgments

This book is about my tour of duty with the 174th ordnance detachment (AR) in Cam Ranh Bay, Vietnam. The detachment was part of the 191st Ordnance Battalion that supplied ammunition to Central Vietnam during the Vietnam War. There are no battles described here, no screaming wounded, no medals awarded for valor. The men I served with were just doing what they were trained to do by an army who said their job was something that needed to be done. I think it is a story that needs telling, and our contribution was an important part of the war.

Were we shot at on a daily basis? Nope, and we did not hump the boonies, nor did we sleep in foxholes. We slept in barracks—if you can call them that—and had bunks and clean clothes if we wanted them, and we ate chow in mess halls. But that does not mean our lives were easy or uneventful. We worked long hours and we worked hard.

Many people helped me in writing this book. I would like to thank my friend, Chris Opie, who urged me to start writing down all the stories I used to tell her. My high school classmate, Gay Machado, whose advice and support through the long process of writing this book were invaluable to me, was that connection to another world during my tour, although she did not know it, and the one who convinced me I could do this. My friend Paul Masterson, who was always available to serve as a friendly critic of my writing, and offer tips on what he thought was right and also what was wrong. Alicia I. Gutierrez, for all the encouragement and positive thoughts. Most of all, I would to thank my editor, Laura Meehan, for her hard work and thoughtful insights.

To the best commanding officer I had in the Army, CWO4 Vern Mello (retired), who was and always will be "Mr. Mello" to the men of the 174thOrdnance Detachment, and to the men who labored in obscurity during the war while humping 150-pound boxes of ammo under a brutal Southeast Asian sun, who worked with explosives while surrounded by thousands of tons of the same, and who never received recognition for their service and all their hard work, I dedicate this book.

I have tried to tell about life as I experienced it during my tour. If I do not come across as particularly heroic, that's OK. That is not what this book is about. It is about what I saw during my tour, not how I should have acted, or what I should have done.

One

Getting There

WELCOME TO VIETNAM

The door opened and the weather I would live with for the next year flooded into the plane. It was September 22, 1968. After an agonizing twenty-two-hour flight from Travis Air Force Base in California, oppressive heat and humidity welcomed me to Bien Hoa, Vietnam. They felt like a warm and humid embrace.

Serving as the unofficial reception committee were the vets who had done their time and were going home on the very plane that had brought me to this hellhole. The taunts and catcalls as we walked past them and were herded onto buses only served to make the coming year seem longer, if that were possible.

Even after we arrived at our permanent duty station, our brand new fatigues would shout FNG's (Fuckin' New Guys). A short-timer could not resist coming up to us and saying, "Seven days, mother-fucker"; since we still had almost the whole year to go in country, it just made the time seem interminable.

The sights and smells of Vietnam assaulted us on our way to the Ninetieth Replacement Battalion at Long Binh: dirt streets, children smoking, *mamasan* urinating along the side of the road, swirling clouds of dust, men holding hands, the ever-present smell of burning feces and urine mixed with diesel fuel.

The driver said the screens over the windows were to stop grenades from being thrown into the bus. Kind of like, "Welcome to Vietnam, a place you can die anyplace, at anytime, any way." That I could be killed before actually getting to the replacement battalion had never occurred to me. I could not imagine being killed within minutes of arriving. If the replacements were in danger of being killed, what the hell was the rest of the goddamn country like? I suppose it gave everyone a taste of what was to come.

My memories of Long Binh are mostly of helicopters and dirt. It seemed helicopters flew over us at least every thirty seconds or so, every model imaginable, going every direction of the compass. The red soil, too, was very pervasive stuff. Some of the paperwork I saved from those days is still stained with it.

We were taken to a barracks and shown bunks where we could sleep, if we were so inclined—few of us did. The beds were just mattresses with mattress covers on them. Those covers were so dirty that some of us refused to lay on them. I'm not talking kind of dirty; I mean encrusted with dirt. I choose to sleep outside with my duffle bag as a pillow rather than sleep on those mattress covers. It was just a new-guy reaction. If I had been returning home through Long Binh, the filth wouldn't have been worth a second look. After a year of never being clean, I wouldn't have thought a filthy mattress cover was a big deal.

The funny thing is that I can remember most of the details I had to do in Long Binh and some of the people involved, but I cannot remember ever going to a mess hall and eating chow. I was there for a week and would have eaten three meals a day, but I remember none of them. When I reported for duty in Vietnam I had been in the Army eleven months and I was a spec four, so I had plenty of experience with Army mess halls, and Army chow. If the meals had been exceptionally bad or good, it seems I would have remembered. So the chow must have been typical Army chow, bland and forgettable.

Some of the incongruities only the Army could have thought up. We had to brush our teeth with a fluoride mixture that looked, tasted, and was the consistency of ready-mix cement. And to top it all off, we could not spit it out—we had to hold the vile stuff in our mouths for a very long time. It seems strange they were worried about our teeth while we could've died any minute from a myriad of causes. But maybe they wanted us to have stronger teeth so we would not go on sick call and could keep killing and being killed. But I will admit the stuff seemed to really help my teeth.

The EM (Enlisted Man) Club at Long Binh was a scene of alcohol-fueled angst as could be expected of men far from home, facing the unknown. Loud music blasted over the speakers, making normal speech impossible. A projector showed a movie depicting a B-52 strike blasting some unknown jungle somewhere. Nothing like death and destruction set to music. It seemed surreal to watch a movie like that while sitting in Vietnam. Since everyone was drinking, it was a pretty disorderly bunch; the sentiment was "we who are about to die."

One guy had been assigned to the 173rd Airborne Division, and it seemed he could not wait. He kept yelling he was going to the "173rd gook killers" at the top of his lungs. I have always wondered what happened to him. Hopefully he did not get the tables turned on him.

Twice a day, there was a formation out in front of the barracks. The cadre would call out the last four numbers of a GI's serial number. If they hollered out yours, then you would go and find out where they were sending you. I always assumed that I would work at the job I was trained to do, my MOS (Military Occupational Specialty). Never even gave it a thought that I might end up doing something else. But of course I had never been in a war before, where warm bodies are one of the biggest supply shortages.

If for some reason there was no need for his specific MOS, then a GI might find himself shipped off to an infantry outfit. Protest was useless, since everyone had been to basic training, not called BCT (Basic Combat Training) for nothing. And just about everyone was given a week of RVN (Republic of Vietnam) training before leaving the states. So the theory was that we were more or less combat trained if we had completed basic and RVN training. Of course everyone knew that was BS, and in reality it was a death sentence for a clerk or mechanic who was unlucky enough to be there on the wrong day. But hey, the quota was filled. This very thing happened to an NCO (Non Commissioned Officer) I knew. Although he was an ammunition specialist, he spent months out in the bush before writing his congressmen, who eventually got him transferred out of the infantry. He had complained to the unit's first sergeant about knowing nothing about being in the infantry, but the first sergeant's only comment was, "You'll learn." It always gave us such a warm feeling when the people in charge really cared about our welfare.

Meanwhile, an interesting switch happened in the 174th during my tour. There were not enough trained ammunition people in the replacement battalions for us, so they sent men who had been trained to be infantrymen to my unit. Now is that weird or what? We couldn't believe it. The commanding officer explained to them that they would never be promoted to sergeant because they had no training in ordnance. Most of them were more than satisfied to stay and not be out in the bush.

FLOWER BEDS OF BIEN HOA (LONG BINH)

It took about a week to get processed in and receive my permanent duty station assignment. Now, everyone who has been in the service knows that during that week, you couldn't just sit around. If your name was not called for assignment, then the Army would find something for you to do: details.

We would be sent out in groups to do things no one else had time to do, or that no one else wanted to do. One job we spent several days on was sorting field gear—ponchos, ammo pouches, packs, web gear, and other assorted equipment. Since the stuff was really mangled, I asked the short, dumpy NCO who was watching us work, "Hey Sarge, where did this stuff come from?"

Giving me a sneering look reserved for FNGs, he said, "All this gear came in from the field, and let's just say that the former owners no longer need field gear where they are headed." I got a sinking feeling in my stomach when he added, "Yeah, that's right—they were KIA."

After being told its former owners were killed, we began handling the gear with a little more reverence. No one wanted to look close enough to see blood stains. Whether he was telling the truth or lying just to scare us, I don't know, but if the latter, it worked—we were certainly scared.

After I had been there a few days, a staff sergeant took four or five other men and me over to the BOQ (Bachelor Officer Quarters). He showed us a pile of lumber, some nails, and what looked like a skinny hatchet (there was no hammer) and explained that he wanted us to build flower beds in front of the building. Now, when I received my orders for Vietnam, I had imagined all kinds of things happening—being killed or wounded, coming down with some dread disease, or maybe getting a medal for some heroic act—but never in my wildest imagination did I see myself building flower beds.

We all just sat there momentarily, dumb looks on our faces, and one guy said, "You want us to build what?" Kind of like a group "Huh?" With a patronizing look on his face, he patiently explained again what he wanted, and build flower beds we did.

The stupid hatchet he had given me was only about an eighth of an inch thick, and it was very difficult to hit the nail squarely with it. Watching me struggle, the staff sergeant asked me where I was from, and I said, "California," and he said, "That figures." Apparently pounding nails with a narrow hatchet was something everyone learned at an early age wherever he was from. Probably someplace with no running water and where everyone married their first cousins, I thought angrily.

What we did not know was a Special Forces (Green Beret) major was listening to our conversation. He said, "You know, Sergeant, my parents are from California." That staff sergeant did not know what to say; his patronizing look was gone, replaced by an, "Oh crap, what have I done now?" look, as he stammered an apology. And we all said under our breath, "Fucking lifer." But at least he left us alone after that, and we went ahead and built the flower beds. I have always wondered where the flowers were going to come from; in the course of my whole tour, I never saw even one flower, much less a Vietnamese Home Depot.

When I received my orders for my permanent duty station, I went by bus back to Bien Hoa Airport to fly up to Cam Ranh Bay. It was great to get out of the mud and dirt of Long Binh. While we were getting on the plane, a C-130, I bumped into the same Special Forces major. For the flight up to Nha Trang, he had to straddle my boots while sitting on the floor of the plane. I always wished that I had found out his name or introduced myself, but I held back; spec fours did not have conversations with majors. I hope he made it back home OK.

Two

Castles in the Sand

BARRACKS LIFE

We were lucky at Cam Ranh Bay in that we had barracks to stay in. No matter how flimsy they were, they were better than tents. Each building was just a frame covered with a nylon screen and one-by-four boards that were set as louvers for the first five feet or so up from the floor.

Blast shields of sand bags about three feet high were set up around the barracks. I can't imagine how they would have protected us from anything the enemy had in their inventory. Like many things, they looked nice, but did not work very well.

The barracks were infested with rats and cockroaches, even though there was poison set out everywhere. Nothing edible could be left out uncovered overnight or it would be eaten by the rats or full of cockroaches the next morning. In our feeble attempts to rid ourselves of these pests, we would set traps for them, the roaches especially.

People often got cookies in care packages from home, packed in two-pound coffee cans—the only way to ship anything so it would not get crushed. After the cookies were eaten and just crumbs re-

Be it ever so humble...my barracks.

mained in the can, we would set it out overnight, and the next morning it would be full of cockroaches. We would take the can, squirt lighter fluid into it, and set it on fire. On a hot and humid Vietnam morning, there was nothing like the smell of cockroaches roasting on an open fire. It was not unusual to walk by on the way to morning formation and see a coffee can sitting out in front of a barracks with black smoke boiling out of it; you could hear those roaches crackling in the fire from the boardwalk.

Now, our roaches were not your everyday cockroaches—they were big, up to three inches long, and they could fly like birds. They would fly around at night and land on you and run up your leg or arm—or, as happened to me on several occasions, your face. I used to sleep with my arm hanging over the side of my bunk, but the roaches seemed to think my arm was the perfect landing strip. So they would fly through the barracks and land on my arm and run up to my shoulder. Did you know roaches have really scratchy feet? To this day, I am unable to sleep with my arm hanging outside my bed, even though it was over forty years ago.

One memorable night, I was sleeping when a roach landed on my leg and ran up to my chest. Jumping out of bed, I grabbed a shower shoe and tried to smash the offender, cussing a streak all the while. I happened to look up, and there stood my friend Spec Four Johnson, who was serving as CQ (Charge Of Quarters) that night. Johnson, who normally looked like a laid-back California surfer dude, looked overtaken by fright.

"Are you all right?" he said.

"Yeah, I was just trying to kill a roach that landed on me."

Later on, he told me he had just been doing his job and walking through the barracks, when I jumped up right in front of him in my attempt to slay the enemy roach. He said he was afraid I had completely lost my mind, another victim claimed by the stress of just being there.

Rats and cockroaches were not the only nighttime visitors to the barracks; there were whores around almost all the time. There was a village nearby, on the Cam Ranh Peninsula, and even though it was off-limits the whole time I was there, the whores still got though the wire. Sometimes they were caught by the MPs, but were soon back, having paid their "fines." Turned out MPs were GIs, just like the rest of us.

One night, a new captain from the Forty-Sixth Ordnance Company was chasing some of them down the boardwalk. He fired his .45 automatic in the air to stop them, scaring the crap out of the sleeping men. The next morning, we complained to our CO, and he said he had already informed the battalion commander about the episode. I am guessing the captain was just being security conscious, because a number of the whores were probably spies, but he could have killed a GI, and he may not have survived that kind of incident.

Sometimes I would be having a beer and a smoke with someone, and right next to us someone would be having sex with a whore under a sheet, and we would think nothing of it. Life really was reduced to the lowest common denominator; such was life in Vietnam.

One day, when I had been in the company area and was headed back to the barracks, I came upon a couple of men crouching by one of the many fire barrels, fifty-five gallon drums painted red, standing in front of the buildings. Since there was no running water in the barracks, these barrels were full of water to be used in case of fire, and each had a couple of buckets hanging on it.

For some reason, probably some obscure Army regulation, the phrase "non potable water" needed to be written on the barrels. I cannot imagine anyone being tempted to take a swig of the evil brew, which consisted of rainwater and whatever else had been thrown in or fallen in. Certainly no GI would have. The only other people around were Vietnamese, and most of them could not read Vietnamese, much less English—but it was doubtful that even they would have wanted to give it a try.

Despite this, the CWO (Chief Warrant Officer), Mr. Mello, had to put out the order for the barrels to be so labeled. Being the intelligent man that he was—and still is—Mr. Mello did not think to ask the men detailed to do the deed if they knew how to spell "potable." He just told them to get a stencil and get busy.

When I showed up, I happened to glance at their handiwork and noticed that they had stenciled "Non Portable Water" onto the barrels. When I pointed out their spelling error, they did not believe me. I told them the correct spelling was "potable," not "portable."

Thinking I was pretty funny, I laughed, "Wow, must be some pretty heavy shit, if it's non portable. If the water is that heavy, maybe you guys can sell it to a nuclear weapons facility."

This comment of course, was returned with any of number smears

CWO Vern Mello at the 174th.

concerning me and my ancestry, the kindest of which was, "Mac, you think you are so fucking smart." I said, "No, I don't think I'm all that smart, but I sure as hell know how to spell 'potable,' and that is not it." But they did not believe me, and would not change the spelling, no matter what I said.

So, from then on, we had non portable water in the 174th Ordnance Detachment. At least it was worth a chuckle every time I walked down the boardwalk in front of the barracks. Never did find out what Mr. Mello thought, though I imagine he probably just shook his head and walked on.

****

The monsoon season in Southeast Asia is a time of being wet and miserable, and it is a fact of life that nothing is ever dry then. If, during the day, your fatigues got wet, they never dried, only stayed kind of damp. The house girls would wash clothes, but you would put them on still damp because they never dried. If you wanted dry cigarettes then you bought a plastic container for the pack; if you didn't, you had damp smokes. Since it rained every day, the sands of Cam Ranh Bay could not absorb all the water, and large puddles pooled everywhere.

An especially large puddle in front of my barracks grew to the size of a small pond. One night, during a really hard rain, the sand dam containing it gave way. When I happened to wake up to go to the latrine, I swung my feet out of my bunk and found I was standing in about six inches of water. The water was running in the front door and out the back. I hollered and woke everyone, and we hit the lights to see beer and soda cans, shower shoes, and everything else floating along in the current.

Everyone quickly put their footlockers up on something to keep them dry, along with their boots, and after this was done, we all went back to sleep. Looking back, it seems strange that with a creek running in the front door and out the back, we just went back to bed. I guess it shows how sleep-deprived we were. Curiously, this was the only time in my whole tour when mosquitoes were a problem—they drove us nuts the rest of the night.

The next morning we had a monumental cleanup job ahead of us, getting rid of all the mud that had washed in. It was the first time I used a shovel to clean up a barracks and my area. No real damage was done; it was just an inconvenience for all involved, making a miserable time and place even worse.

One night, Mr. Mello showed up in the barracks with a determined look on his face, searching for a particular GI who shall remain nameless. Turned out this GI had never written to his mother since shipping out to Vietnam, and she called the Red Cross, thinking the worst. Anyway, Mr. Mello located the missing GI and took him by the arm. Anytime a commanding officer showed up looking for you, it was not a good thing, and the look on the GI's face reflected his concern.

Mr. Mello escorted him to the orderly room, sat him down at his desk, gave him a pen and some paper, and told him, "Write your mother a letter"—which he apparently did to Mr. Mello's satisfaction, because it never happened again. That was the only time I ever saw someone in the Army get a direct order to write to his mom.

Toward the end of my tour, we had a company meeting one night—the reason escapes me—and we were all sitting around the kind of club we had put together. When the meeting was over and people were starting to leave, there was suddenly a huge explosion. A column of flames at least a hundred feet high shot up from out behind our shower building. I'm sure everyone's heart was in his throat, figuring we were under some sort of attack. We all rushed downstairs to see what happened. Turned out that a pipeline carrying JP-4 jet fuel had exploded behind our company area.

We had a good time watching the Vietnamese firemen trying to put out the fire. All they did was get their trucks stuck in the sand, and then the fire went out after the valves were shut off, cutting off the fuel in the pipeline.

We were told that the explosion was caused by a rupture in the pipe that caused the fuel to explode. I don't think anyone believed that story; it had to be sabotage. The pipeline was easy to see, since it was above ground. It had probably originally been buried, but the wind had blown the sand away. And as far as I know, there were never any patrols along the line—at least I never saw any. It would have been simple for any of the Vietnamese around to put a device on the pipeline.

****

For my birthday in 1969, I received a care package from home. Inside was a cake my mom had made for me. Now, that may seem like no big thing, but this cake was still a cake. Prior to this, many

View across the bay from where the jet fuel pipeline exploded. Burn mark is visible just right of the shed.

men had received cakes, but they were always just crumbs in the corners of their boxes. Nothing that even resembled a cake had ever made it through the mail.

My mom must have hit the mail just right, and the cake made its way to me within a couple of days. Mom had even put in the right number of candles: twenty-two. So, that night, I gathered all my friends around, and we all had birthday cake, after I blew out the candles of course. The cake was chocolate on chocolate, and it was the best. We were always starved for sweets, and this cake satisfied everyone's sweet tooth. My mom was everyone's favorite mom that day.

****

The darker side of barracks life was the disagreements that were bound to happen with so many people living together—especially with alcohol available and used to excess. It helped that we all quickly figured out who to avoid when they were drinking. If I walked into a barracks and saw certain people drinking, I would just turn around and leave. Of course, that is not to say nothing ever went wrong.

One of the most savage fights I have ever witnessed took place one evening after chow. I didn't know the two combatants or even where they were from or why they were fighting, but they went at each other with a viciousness that was amazing even for Vietnam. By the time the fight ended, there must have been two hundred men watching. Fortunately I was not an NCO then, and didn't feel obligated to try and break it up.

The two men appeared to be fighting to the death, and refused to stop, no matter what got in their way. One man picked up a piece of four by four and beat the other with it. Since he used the corner of the board, it left dents in the other brawler. I had never known a body could be dented. The other man picked up a neon light tube and broke it across his opponent's back. Needless to say, this was a bloody thing to watch. Finally an NCO heard the ruckus and broke up the fight before someone was beaten to death. Just another day in paradise, I suppose.

At one point, a directive came down that said we were to turn in all entrenching tools, which consisted of a shovel with a pick on the other end. We had all been issued one when we got to our duty stations. Apparently too many men were using them as weapons, and killing other GIs with them. I wondered which was preferred as a weapon, the pick or the shovel? It was not a big deal for us, since we didn't have to dig foxholes with them anyway. The only thing I had ever used mine for was filling sandbags.

I doubt that, for the want of an entrenching tool, anyone's life was saved. I certainly didn't feel any better knowing no one around me had an entrenching tool handy. If one of us wanted to kill someone, we certainly had the tools to do it. I mean, we had access to real weapons, like guns and explosives. But orders were orders, so we all turned the tools in. The confiscation of entrenching tools from a few GIs at Cam Ranh Bay was kind of a Band-Aid approach to the problem of GIs murdering each other. I don't remember anything being done to lessen the boredom, isolation, drinking, and all around bad behavior.

Every company had its practical jokers, usually doing things like short-sheeting beds, yelling attentions when entering the barracks, and tying boot laces together. But we had one of the best: Delk, from Mississippi, who could throw his voice. Somehow he could talk deep down in his throat and make it sound like someone was hollering for you from far away. He tried it on me one time, and he had me going for a few minutes, but I happened to turn around and catch him in the act, spoiling his fun. It was especially fun to watch him do it to someone who'd had one too many beers.

One night, Delk had a sergeant first class from the 46th Ordnance running from one end of the company area to the other, looking for whomever was calling for him. It's a wonder he did not have a heart attack. We were all laughing so hard, I thought one of us might have a heart attack. Every new guy that came into the detachment got the treatment from Delk sooner or later..

****

All the time I was in Vietnam, housegirls did our laundry and cleaned up our areas. They were not whores, at least not in my company. They washed clothes, swept the barracks, and would even iron your fatigues if you wanted. Some places, they would even shine men's boots, but our housegirls thought that was above and beyond their duties.

In Vietnam, number one is the best and number ten is the worst. I mention this, because one time I noticed that my handkerchiefs were slowly disappearing, and I wondered why. I mentioned this to my housegirl, Thom, and she told me she had been rating them. She said that, if I had just wiped sweat with a handkerchief, then it was a number one, but if I had blown my nose on it, then it was a number ten, and she would throw it away. I said, "What do you mean you throw them away?" Somewhere between angry and resigned, I pointed out, "It's your job to do the laundry, not pick and choose what you will or won't wash." But it did no good; she would not wash them. That's when I changed housegirls, and Mai replaced Thom.

Being rear area troops, we were required to look half decent every day, and that included being cleanly shaven. Whether with cold water or hot, shaving was something that had to be done, and for most people it was no big thing, just a pain in the butt. But we had one man, Seymour, who could not shave with a regular razor, as the process gave him ingrown whiskers. The only remedy was some concoction that he would smear on his face and then scrape off with a kitchen knife. Unfortunately, the stuff smelled like roadkill—really old roadkill. I can still remember being in the shower room, and someone would say, "Oh shit, here comes Seymour. Hurry up!" Everyone would finish as fast as they could so as to be gone when he started shaving. Must have been great for Seymour; he always had the shower room to himself and never had to wait to shower or shave.

All NCOs in the 174th had private rooms, and to cure "loneliness," they would sometimes keep girls in their rooms. Now, this was frowned upon by the powers that be, and strictly against the rules. But it was done all the time, and as long as no one complained, it was kind of overlooked.

Well, one sergeant I knew, who shall remain nameless, had a guest, and for some reason an NCO from a different company in the barracks next door saw her and turned him in to the MPs—he was probably jealous. Hearing a jeep pull up, my friend looked out the window and saw that the MPs were on their way up to his room. It was too late to get his guest out, so he put her in his duffle bag and told her to be quiet. This would have been hard even for your average Vietnamese woman, so she must have been a small economy-size model.

Pretending to be asleep when the MPs knocked, he let them in and they searched the room and found nothing. As they were leaving the room, the duffle bag fell over and the girl let out a yell. I think everyone can imagine the questioning look on the MPs' faces, and the sickly grin on my friend's. Of course, the girl was terrified too, because she didn't want to be turned over to the Vietnamese police, the "White Mice." A lot of things might happen to her then, and none of them were good. Since my friend was close to going home, he was not prosecuted, but he did not get several awards he had been due to receive. Mr. Mello had used his considerable pull to get the prosecution stopped—that is why the men of the 174th had so much respect for him. He took care of us.

THE PHANTOM

Cam Ranh Bay, Vietnam: The Dry Season, 1969

I awoke in my bunk. I thought, Why am I awake? The hooch was quiet: no one was running through, screaming "Alert!" No whores were around, I didn't hear any explosions—I didn't even have to pee. So what was I doing awake?

My buddy Herzog said, "Hey, Mac, you awake?" and I said, "Yeah."

"Did you see that guy?" he asked. "He ran into your bunk."

Well, at least I knew why I was awake. I answered, "No, I didn't see anything. Why? What happened?"

Thus began the saga of the Phantom of the 174th, some of the weirdest and strangest and most outrageous behavior I ever saw in my days in Vietnam. Let me explain.

My buddy Herzog had been sleeping, and was awakened by a hand fondling him. He looked down, and there was a hand playing with his privates. He looked left and right, could see both of his own hands, but could not figure out where this third hand was coming from. All he could think to say was "BOO!" And the phantom jumped up and ran outside, running into my bunk on the way.

Apparently the phantom would creep into a hooch, get down on his hands and knees alongside his victim's bunk, and then start playing with the occupant's privates. This was made easy by the climate in Cam Ranh Bay, which was hot, even stifling, most of the time. Once the wet season was over, no one slept under covers. We just lay on top of the bunks in our underwear. This gave plenty of opportunity for the phantom to play out his fantasies, or whatever he was doing.

He struck a number of times in one of our company's barracks, the one next to mine. One night, another GI grabbed him and screamed for someone to hit the lights. But the phantom pulled loose and got away, which probably kept him alive to fondle again. It is amazing how the imminent threat of death can increase a person's strength.

We never found out who this person was or even where he was from. Was he one of us? From the Transportation Company next door? Or maybe from the Signal Company across the parking area? Nobody seemed to know.

I have always wondered what drove him. What kind of compulsion did he have, to make him fondle strange men in their bunks? Was he hoping someone would like it and ask him to stay? And trust me, he was risking his life to do it. People started getting paranoid, and put trip wires attached to cans around their bunks to try and catch him. But the attacks tapered off and then stopped. So we never found out who the Phantom of the 174th was, or what happened to him. Did he DEROS (Date Of Estimated Rotation Overseas) out and go home? Or get himself beaten to death somewhere else? He could have been the phantom of all of Cam Ranh Bay for all I know, and not just the 174th's. His appearance and disappearance remain a mystery.

DID YOU HEAR?

"Did you hear Alling got stabbed?" Von Dran asked me, as I sat on my bunk.

"Who's Alling?" I asked.

"The new guy."

"What new guy?" I had never heard of anyone named Alling.

Turned out he had just arrived in the company the previous day, December 31, 1968. That evening, since he did not know anyone, he had just gone to bed rather than celebrate New Year's Eve.

Several hours later, someone came by and stabbed him. Why? No one knew. Who? No one ever found out. He just had the bad luck to be in the first bunk to the left of the door when the stabber came by. It was a very severe wound, and he spent the first six weeks of his tour in the hospital.

Later on, two other GIs and I looked around and found knife cuts in the blankets and mattresses on the first bunks on the left in the two other barracks as well. Unfortunately for Alling, he was in that first bunk in the third barracks when the attacker came by. Later he told us he thought someone had just punched him, until he saw all the blood.

I don't remember anyone being really surprised that it happened, just curious about who had done it and why. What a place—you get stabbed in bed, and no one is surprised. I was mostly glad it wasn't me, but then again, I was out drinking and carousing, not sleeping.

Why did the stabber stop with one victim? It seemed obvious that whoever it was simply wanted to stab someone. Apparently the one victim satisfied his bloodlust, because it never happened again. It was a pretty strange way to celebrate New Year's Eve, by stabbing a perfect stranger. But in the barracks, even celebrations could get out of hand sometimes. That same night, someone shot a couple of Lima 312 flares horizontally down the whole length of the company area. They went by the door about three feet off the ground, bursting out in the dunes. It is amazing that some GI was not skewered by one of the little rockets. If struck by one, you would be SOL for sure.

As far as I can remember, neither incident was ever investigated. After a while, Alling came back to the company, and just became known as "the guy who got stabbed."

SHITHOUSES AND PISSTUBES

When I arrived in Vietnam and started down the gangway from the airplane, the first thing I noticed after the absolutely oppressive heat and humidity was the columns of black smoke on the horizon. I must have seen at least six to eight columns, just glancing around. Fires from attacks, I thought.

It did not take long to find out that these columns of smoke were from the burning of waste. In Vietnam, all solid waste was burned. The outhouses, or shithouses, as they were called, were set over cutoff fifty-five gallon drums, which collected all the shit. Later on, some lucky individual would drag the drums out, fill them partway up with diesel fuel, and set the contents on fire—hence the columns of black smoke.

I don't suppose I need to describe the smell of burning diesel fuel and shit; it has an aroma all its own. I am sure that smell is ingrained in all Vietnam vets' memories. Every once in a while, the burning would take place in the evening when almost everyone was in the barracks, and if the wind was just right, it would blow all the soot into the barracks. Since it always hot and humid, the soot would stick to everything and everyone it came in contact with. You have never heard a bunch of GIs swear, until you have been in a barracks when burning shit soot drifted in and started sticking to every sweating body. It amazed me that no really serious diseases ended up passed on by that soot.

I don't know about other companies, but ours had a permanent shitburner. He had been kicked out of the ammunition storage areas and the renovation line because he was too careless with the ammunition—he had no fear. Having had to perform this very odious task myself a couple of times, I did not envy him. But the hours were great and there was no real danger involved, and he did not seem to mind it at all. Everyone else was more than happy to have him do the job.

Now, when it came to taking a leak, we had the "pisstubes." These consisted of a five-inch-diameter rocket container about five feet long crammed into the top of a fifty-five gallon drum. The drums were buried and only the container stuck out of the ground. Into this, people would urinate and also discard used condoms and everything else you can imagine. It is not hard to imagine the smell on a humid and very hot Southeast Asian night or day. No one had to give directions to the pisstubes; it was obvious where they were located. I would hate to be the person who happens sometime in the future to dig into one of those old spots where they were buried.

Curiously, in our company, we never thought about putting a roof over the pisstubes. So to use them if it was raining, we had to get wet or wear a poncho, which of course we had to pull up while urinating. Some GIs got lazy and just pissed in front of the barracks if it was raining hard, and of course then the front of the barracks stated to smell like the pisstubes. The CO threatened to give an Article 15 (nonjudicial punishment) to anyone he caught doing this, but it never really stopped.

HAS THE WAR STARTED YET?

Cam Ranh Bay was a fairly safe place, mainly because of geography. The bay was just too wide for most of the weapons in the enemy's arsenal to reach us. But I am sure they used to sit across the bay in those mountains, in that stinking jungle, and watch us watching movies with all the depots all lit up, and salivate, thinking about how great it would be if they could kill every one of us.

But in addition to the geography, Cam Ranh was guarded by the South Korean Army, mainly the White Horse Division. The South Koreans had a reputation for being ruthless; this and their reputation as fighters made for a pretty safe area.

When I was on R&R, I met a GI that was stationed on an artillery base. He told me that when the South Koreans who guarded the base captured a housegirl who was carrying the plans for the base on her person, after questioning her for a time, they just shot her—problem solved. That sort of attitude had a way of getting around, and invoking fear is a twisted sort of control. As far as I know, no U.S. ground troops were stationed around Cam Ranh. The only infantry I ever observed were South Korean and South Vietnamese.

But scary reputations or not, the VC (Viet Cong) or NVA (North Vietnamese Army), still gave it the old college try every once in a while, so we had a ringside seat to the war. It was like going to the drive-in movies. If the action looked pretty interesting, we would drag our lawn chairs out and grab a beer and cigarettes and sit down and watch the war. Nothing like having a tall cool one while people are dying.

We could hear and see the explosions and watch the tracer rounds fly through the air and ricochet off into the darkness, winking out like demented fireflies. We'd watch the helicopter gunships firing their machine guns and the flares drifting along on the wind. Of course, we had learned that an alert would eventually be called if the action went on too long, so we might as well go back and get ready to be called out.

During the day we could sometimes observe jets making bombing runs on the mountains and listen to the dull thud of their bombs exploding seconds later. It was strange, like being in a war, but not really, experiencing combat vicariously. So we would sit there in our lawn chairs, drinking our beer and smoking cigarettes, watching the war and feeling glad we were not in the middle of it.

As the men in the rear with the gear, we got to see all the new stuff (ammo, guns, tanks, and the like) when it came into the country. Once I saw a new Sheridan tank on a flatbed truck, heading up-country in all its glory, looking formidable with its large gun and armor, the very symbol of our power. And then I saw the same kind of tank a couple of weeks later, dirty and smashed, looking dejected on a trailer heading the other way, back to the States for scrap.

We used to pass by an area that in the States would be called a junkyard. I don't remember what it was called over there, but it was a kind of salvage yard, where they brought all the smashed and mangled tanks, trucks, APCs (Armored Personnel Carriers), jeeps—every type of vehicle used in Vietnam. It was sobering to see all those vehicles wrecked, battered, demolished, and blasted—just like the men who had been in them.

One day, someone brought an AK-47 into one of our shops, and we were all examining it. After everyone else had left, I was playing around with it, trying to figure how to fieldstrip it—which, by the way, was very easy. No wonder it is such a popular gun around the world; anyone can use the darn thing.

The unfortunate person who had been in possession of the AK-47 had been killed, it was said. It was easy to believe, since the gun's stock and forearm had a number of bullet holes in them. As I taught myself the art of fieldstripping an AK-47, I removed the forearm and found the space in between the barrel and wood was full of some kind of gunk. I proceeded to clean it out, not thinking about what it might be. It was not until I found several pieces of bone that it dawned on me what I was dealing with. Someone's finger bone and rotten flesh was what I had been cleaning out and throwing on the floor. An "Oh shit" moment if there ever was one. We may have seen the beginning of many pieces of equipment's useful lives, and seen what they looked like at the end, but every once in a while, the middle reared its ugly head and showed us what war really was like.

We had a pistol in our shop made out of a three-quarter-ton truck's door handle. It looked like it might fire the round for a .32 automatic or something similar. But it was a functioning weapon, and we were amazed that anyone could have come up with the idea to build it. It made us wonder what else the VC had made just using some of our scrap metal.

"I'LL BURY YOU"

When the three-quarter ton Army truck drove through the company area, closely followed by a covey of MP jeeps, with a colonel firing a .45 automatic at the truck, I knew I was in trouble with a capital T—and I was right.

A half hour before, I had been on CQ, minding my own business, just another spec four doing what he was told to do. I was in my first month of a twelve-month tour.

A new guy named Rogers came into the orderly room and wanted to borrow the keys to one of the trucks. He and some others wanted to go down to the Village on Cam Ranh Bay—which we always called "the Vill"—and try to pick up some whores to bring back to the company area.

This was against policy, and at first, since I was CQ and in charge of the company area, I said no. However, Rogers finally whined at me enough and, against my better judgment, I said yes, he could take the keys to one of the two-and-a-half-ton trucks. Little did I know that my stupid decision could have cost me my life.

Unbeknownst to me, Rogers also took the keys to one of the three-quarter-ton trucks. The whore run was a common practice among many companies at Cam Ranh, and no one thought much of it. But I guess it had come to the attention of the MPs, and they wanted to put a stop to it. Having set up a roadblock right in front of the Vill, they were stopping all vehicles and checking out why they were there. Well, our whore-hunting "ammo humpers" (slang for anyone who worked in the storage areas) panicked and ran the roadblock, and that's when the fun really started.

When they blasted through the roadblock, they apparently came really close to running over one of the MP colonels. Of course he took this very personally and took off after the offending truck. It was quite the show while it lasted, as the convoy of vehicles raced all around Cam Ranh Post, with the colonel at point.

After a few circuits around the post, Sergeant Jones, who was driving the three-quarter ton, gave up and stopped the truck. He was arrested by the MPs and taken to their headquarters. Of course, they called our CO after all this excitement, and he came down to the company area. Since Sergeant Jones was to go home in a few days, our CO, Mr. Mello, was able to have him freed without charges, and he did not go to jail. No one was given a court martial or even an Article 15, which really surprised me. Whatever Mr. Mello did, it must have been pretty special.

After everything calmed down, Mr. Mello came to see me, and wanted to know how Rogers and Jones came to have the keys, for the trucks. Before I answered, he gave me a little speech. What he said was, "If you are lying to me, and I find out about it later, I will bury you." I understood that, translated, this meant he would see to it that I was transferred to an infantry unit, where it was almost certain I would be killed. Ordnance types like me did not last long out in the boonies.

He gave me a few minutes to think about it, and then asked me for my answer. I decided to tell the truth; I told him what I had done and what keys I had given out. He asked again, "Is that the truth?" and I said yes. He said, "If that is true, then I will never mention it again," and he never did.

But I never forgot, and in this case, the truth really did set me free.

THANKSGIVING 1968

I had been looking forward to Thanksgiving Day for ages; turkey with all the trimmings sure sounded good. Day of, however, when we got back to the company area from the ammo storage areas and were heading for the mess hall that we shared with the 33rd Ordnance Company, First Sergeant Fisher approached me and asked me to follow him. He explained to me that I had some extra duty that evening: I was going to help search the Vietnamese workers at the ferry terminal.

Ferry terminal? I hadn't even known there was such a thing, but orders were orders, so I grabbed a ride down to the port and found the ferry terminal. I reported to the MPs, who dutifully checked my name from their roster and told me what my duties would be. I was to search all the Vietnamese workers' bags to make they did not steal anything from the base.

So, for the next two hours or so, I confiscated towels, cans of C-rations, P-38 can openers, and some personal articles. I also ran across a lot of fresh food, but I let most of that go through. After a couple of hours, I was cut loose, and I headed back to the company area and chow.

I approached the chow hall and, once there, spoke to a cook about my Thanksgiving dinner. I was informed there was nothing left and if I wanted anything to eat I could have a liverwurst sandwich. *Well, so much for my buddies saving me something.* I told the cook I would rather go hungry than have a liverwurst sandwich for Thanksgiving and went back to my barracks with no dinner. I felt like the only GI in Vietnam that did not get a Thanksgiving Dinner. Hell, Thanksgiving was probably even being served to the prisoners in LBJ (Long Binh Jail), the main stockade in Vietnam, which was affectionately called by the initials of the president who had sent most of us to Vietnam.

The next day, still in a foul mood about missing Thanksgiving dinner, I was sent down to the ferry terminal to search the Vietnamese workers again. When I arrived, the MP in charge said, "Damn, Specialist, what did you do wrong to get this two days in a row?" I didn't know, and never did find out what I did to deserve the extra duty that made me miss my Thanksgiving dinner. As far as I knew, no one else in the company ever had to do that duty as long as I was there. I was even more pissed after the MP's comment, and most of the workers got a free pass that night and got to keep most of their stolen goods. Hopefully they did not have anything that could have hurt anyone, because I sure didn't look for it.

SOMETHING TO CALL THEIR VERY OWN

During my tenure in Vietnam with the 174th Ordnance Detachment, no Vietnamese people were allowed to use the shithouses. This was not a racial issue; it was because of their method of using the facilities. Apparently they thought it was improper to sit on toilet seats, and preferred to squat. We never figured out if this was a cultural thing or what. But their aim wasn't always very good, and they ended up crapping on the seat. And whoever had shit-burning duty objected to having to clean human waste off of the toilet seats. Can't say that I can blame them for not wanting that duty; I mean, shit-burning duty was onerous enough without that kind of nonsense. Thus the housegirls were banished to the bushes out behind the showers. Makes me wonder what they would have done if there were no bushes back there—or should I say, what we would have done.

Well, one day, when a group of us were sitting around the barracks, someone had the idea of making a Vietnamese shithouse. Those of us present thought that was a pretty good idea. If they had their own facility, maybe it would improve their aim and they could stay out of the bushes.

So we scrounged up some lumber, and built them their own little one-holer shithouse. The shitburner said he would burn it if they could hit it. But alas, it did no good; they still crapped on the seat and no one would clean up the mess, neither them nor us. So we tore it apart and used the lumber for something else, and so, once again, the housegirls were banished to the bushes behind the shower building. Sounds kind of cruel, but what could we do? Certainly not change their personal habits, because we tried that. I suppose this whole misunderstanding stemmed from the fact that Vietnamese toilets were just holes in the ground, and there was nothing to sit on.

The lack of facilities never seemed bother many locals around Cam Ranh. We had grown used to seeing locals urinate alongside the road when we were across the bay. It was common to see some *mamasan* walking along the side of the road and, if the urge hit her, just squatting and letting it fly. Since most people wore silk pants with really wide legs, it was a simple operation to pull one leg up to their crotches and do the deed. The fact that they would not sit on a toilet but would urinate alongside the road in full view of everyone passing by was something none of us could quite figure out.

Of course, children seemed to have a license to urinate or crap anywhere. I remember watching a father leaning on a shovel, patiently waiting for his child to crap in the dirt next to the road so he could cover it up. Sights like that took some getting used to, and did not help the reputation of the Vietnamese among many GIs, who seemed to think that being called a third-world country would be a step up for Vietnam. This was one example of the racism that tended to result when the two cultures clashed.

SMOKING, DRINKING, AND DRUGS

A couple of years ago, I ran across my old ration card from Vietnam, and I noticed that most of the months were punched out for cigarettes. We were allowed six cartons a month, which is a lot of cigarettes—six hundred. How I managed to smoke all those cigarettes in a month is beyond me. But at least the price was right: $1.40 a carton, or $.14 a pack. And that was for the premium brands; you could buy other brands for as little as $.80 a carton.

Doing the math, I could never figure how some people I worked with never seemed have money for smokes; they were always bumming cigarettes. Good grief, they could have maxed out their ration card for less than $10, but I ended up giving away a good portion of my ration to my smokeless friends. At least, that's what I assume happened, since I can't imagine having the time to smoke all those cigarettes.

Alcohol was another thing that was really cheap: $3 a case for beer and $2.50 a bottle for booze. Other brands could be less, as cheap as a $1 a case for something like Brown Derby beer. Sodas were even cheaper than beer; Shasta cost $2.40. So most people drank a lot of beer, and everyone drank a lot of sodas, since the water tasted so horrible. The only time we ever drank water was when we were working in the storage areas or on guard, when we did not have access to anything else.

The only problem with all the cheap alcohol was when it was combined with all the easily accessible weapons. After all, this was a war; everyone had access to a weapon. There is nothing like living with a bunch of heavily armed drunks to make your day. But, curiously, at least in my company, though there were plenty of drunken incidents, no one was shot. Maybe it was because as I mentioned earlier, we all just figured out who to stay away from when they were drinking.

Many equate the Vietnam War with the widespread use of marijuana. You might get the impression that every GI was loaded all the time. But in my company, the users were in a minority, and in fact, most men did not drink or smoke dope or even cigarettes. Despite what was shown on TV in those days, the penalties for being caught with dope were severe. A friend of mine was caught with a pipe full of dope and a bag of dope, but he lucked out since he was almost ready to go home. He was only busted to private E1 and fined. If he had had a long time to go on his tour, he would have ended up in LBJ. And in the Army, stockade time is bad time, and doesn't count toward your tour. So if someone spent four months in LBJ, he spent sixteen months in Vietnam.

One evening, I was visiting a friend of mine who lived next door and was in a signal company. We had actually gone to high school together before winding up next door in Vietnam. What were the odds of that happening?

Anyway, while we were talking, I noticed a pipe sitting on his footlocker. I said, "I didn't know you smoked a pipe"; fact is, I didn't know he smoked at all.

He said, "Yeah, but you know it's a real drag that the seeds keep blocking the smoke at the bottom of the bowl."

He caught me off guard there, and it took me a second to comprehend. I just figured Vietnam had claimed another victim. I said, "Yeah, I bet that's a drag"—no pun intended.

During my tour, I heard rumors of GIs mixing drugs with alcohol and ending up dead. It seems that antidepressants could be bought across the bay with no prescription, and those plus beer added up to death. One night, a guy in my company showed me a pillbox with some pills in it. They were called "Black Bombers," or something like that. Looking at the box, I saw that all the writing was in French—and this guy sure as hell did not read French. I said, "Man you don't even know what you are taking!" But he did not listen. Whether or not he even took them, I don't know. Maybe he should have, because after he went back to the States, he was sent to prison for rape.

ROCKETS

During the summer of 1969, I was lying on my bunk, reading a book. To my left, a group was playing cards—poker, I believe. It was just another hot, stifling night at Cam Ranh Bay—the only place I ever lived where writing a letter would cause you to break a sweat.

Off to the west toward the port, I heard a muffled boom, and then a couple more. I put my book down and looked at the poker players, and they looked at me apprehensively. There was a pause, and then it started again, and this time closer. Finally it dawned on us: "ROCKETS!"

Then, the next salvo hit a lot closer, and they came one after the other. The rockets detonated with blasts that sounded like a door slamming really hard with a terrific explosion right after. We piled out of the barracks and headed to the bunker between the buildings. Just as I hit the door, a rocket exploded not too far away. I could see the shrapnel glowing white hot as it flew through the air.

We all jumped up and headed for the bunkers as fast as we could. The bunkers were just large culvert sections covered with a couple layers of sandbags. They might have given some sort of protection against shrapnel, but absolutely none against a direct hit or even a close miss.

I had remembered to duck on the way to the bunker, but others forgot, and were literally clotheslined, for lack of a better word. The

Vietnamese housegirls had strung clotheslines between the barracks for drying the laundry. Since they were pretty low, the ropes caught many men right underneath the chin as they raced to the bunkers.

We all made it to the bunker, albeit with a few bumps and bruises. I had tripped over a friend who hit the deck when a rocket exploded. Apparently the rockets were aimed for the port, and we just received the overspray. There were no casualties among us or in any other barracks.

A few days later, we saw what a 122 mm rocket can do to a five-ton cargo truck. One had taken a direct hit while waiting at the port to be loaded, and it was not pretty. Both the driver and shotgun were severely wounded but lived, according to our CO.

We spent the rest of the night out on alert, sitting in trucks, waiting for something to happen in the ammo storage areas, under the assumption that they were going to be attacked and that the rockets were just a distraction (some distraction). However, nothing else happened, and all we lost was sleep. Although no one was hurt in the barracks, the rockets had come close enough to scare the hell out of us.

McNAMARA'S ONE HUNDRED THOUSAND

I find it very difficult to write this section. I mean no disrespect or denigration of anyone's service to their country; nor do I want to call anyone stupid or dumb or anything in between.

When I was in Vietnam, I met several men who could not read or write. I found this very puzzling, because when I was drafted, I had to take numerous tests and I could not figure out how they took those tests if they were unable to read or write. But I just chalked it up to the Army being the Army, and figured they found a way around everything.

I also found it odd that I had never met or seen any of those same men in ordnance school at Redstone Arsenal, since many of us re-

Me at the bunker in the company area that held all the basic load of small arms ammunition.

ported to the 174th Ordnance Detachment at almost the same time. It seems like I should have at least seen them at Redstone at some time or another, but I hadn't.

It wasn't until thirty years after leaving the Army that I found out the answers to my questions. Only then, in conversations with my old CO, Vern Mello, I discovered the truth about my observations in Vietnam. Many of these men had been part of McNamara's One Hundred Thousand. Back in the mid-sixties, the standards were dropped so the quotas of men drafted could be sustained. This was a direct result of a memo from the secretary of defense, Robert McNamara.

Vern Mello told me that the plan had been to integrate these men into a company, figuring that the other men, who had actually attended regular ordnance school, would take up the slack. And I guess the plan worked to a certain extent, although I do not know how many of these men were in my company. Since no one was killed and nothing blew up while I was there, I guess the reasoning was correct.

According to Vern, the men had gone to some sort of ordnance school in Texas. Vern knew this firsthand because he was CO of one of the companies. He knew many of the men personally, since he had been their commanding officer at the ordnance school.

It is a good thing I did not know then what I found out later on. If I had known many of the men handling explosives around me had never gone to my school, I would not have been very happy—and that's an understatement. Not that there was anything I could have done about it. Anyway, some men were kicked out of their areas, so I guess kind of a natural selection took place, and the really bad ones were weeded out.

We had so much work to do, most of the time we did not have time to get into work that involved actual working knowledge of the ammunition—the type of information we learned in regular ordnance school such as Ammunition Renovation School at Redstone Arsenal, but which I do not think was taught in the abbreviated course. Fortunately, ammunition is all color-coded, so it is pretty simple to learn and remember the basics.

Again, I would not denigrate the service of these men. They went to Vietnam and served honorably when others would not.

HAVE YOU EVER BEEN LONELY?

I'm not sure that "loneliness" is the correct term for what happens in a place like Vietnam, or in the service generally. It's hard when you are left with no choice about what to do, and can only do your duty, with no way out. In our all-male society, there was no room for emotions most of the time, except anger, which there was always plenty of. I always had a sense of being isolated while among a crowd of people.

That loneliness is why the bargirls were so successful: everyone was so starved for affection, for something not male. What was missing was a little tenderness in our lives. It wasn't exactly loneliness. Maybe "despair" is a better term.

The lack of intimacy (not sex), combined with being far from home and living in a very dangerous place where few people could actually be trusted, contributed to my feelings of isolation. Some men couldn't stand it, and it tipped them over the edge.

I felt like no one from back home cared, because, most likely, no one did. We were just "out of sight, out of mind." Of course, most of our parents cared (though not all), but sometimes it felt like everyone was against you, and whether you lived or died was no one else's concern. I think that defined the feeling, the isolation, fear of the unknown, the drudgery of duty.

Sometimes it seemed time really did stand still in Vietnam. Even though we were always busy, there was a lot of down time, and that was the worst: sitting around the barracks with nothing to do, nowhere to go; that's why some men gave alcohol and cigarettes such a workout. When I think back on it, I realize many men were already alcoholics in their early twenties.

We had one man in our unit who just disappeared one morning. They found him a couple of days later, wandering around the Air Force base. They brought him back to the company area to pick up his gear, and we never saw or heard from him again. People said that he had received a Dear John letter from his wife, but we never really knew for sure. Bad news could have that effect, though, since there was nothing we could do from so far away, and no way to get in touch with anyone. Sometimes it felt like we were on another planet; everything was so far away. If there was a real emergency, such as a death in the family, then something would be done. But the powers that be didn't seem to think a straying wife or girlfriend was a good reason for emergency leave. A guy just had to internalize the bad news and try to gut it out—although sometimes it did not work out quite that easily. When the one reason for going home disappeared, some men found daily life difficult to endure.

R & R

Also known as I & I (Intercourse and Intoxication), R & R was something everyone had a chance to experience during their tours. There were many possible destinations to choose from: Thailand, Formosa, Australia, Japan, Malaysia, and Hawaii, among others. You had to spend a certain amount of time in-country to qualify for R & R; I think it was six months.

When we had been in-country long enough, my buddy Elmquist and I decided we needed to go, so we signed up and waited for a slot to open up. At first, we had wanted to go to Malaysia, but it developed a bad case of anti-American riots, and that ended that idea. Then it was Australia. So we waited and waited, but Australia was very popular, and no slots ever opened up. By the time we had both been in-county for nine months, we figured that if we didn't go pretty soon, we might as well not go, since we would be going home before long.

We went and talked to our first sergeant, SFC Fisher, and asked, "What countries are open?" After giving us that "Oh no, not you two again" look, he glanced at his list and said that Japan was open. And we said, "Great, we'll go there!" So that is how we ended up in Japan. We really didn't care where we went; we just wanted out of where we were.

We did all the tourist stuff, going to Ginza, the emperor's palace, Tokyo Tower, Kamakura, and the beach. We had a great time, and I developed a taste for Japanese beer that has lasted to this day. We also found the people to be really friendly and helpful.

Our interpreter and I got along well; he used to live in California too, until he was deported for not going to school like he was supposed to. When we were in our hotel one day, he suddenly said he wanted to go to the Navy base for a steak dinner. I thought it was kind of odd, but I said, "OK, I'll take you." I could get in with my Army ID card.

We had a great dinner while listening to a Japanese band playing country and western songs, pronouncing their Rs as Ls, making me wonder where *home on the lange* was. Years later, I found out how expensive beef was in Japan (along with everything else). The interpreter could not afford it in most places, so that was why he talked me into going to the Navy base. That was OK with me, though—the dinner was great, even if the music was a little weird.

We also enjoyed other luxuries while there. One of the best amenities in the hotel room was the bathtub. It was so deep that the water level was just below my chin. I filled that tub up with the hottest water I could stand and soaked my butt for so long I almost shriveled up. Back at Cam Ranh we considered ourselves lucky that we were safe enough to actually take showers, and if we were not too late, we could get warm ones. The showers were solar heated—who would have thought we would be so green so many years ago? So if we were late, we took cold ones, and sometimes we just used hoses over rafters outside. But either way, we could never spend more than a couple of minutes in the shower, so it was great to be this clean after nine months. I believe "heavenly" was the best term for it.

Unbeknownst to us, while we were making plans for our trip, one of my least favorite people in the company overheard us and signed up to go along on the same flight. And he stuck to us like epoxy glue for the whole damn five days. It wasn't that Von Dran was a bad guy; he was just different. For instance, this was a guy that wrote thirty-page letters to his sister. His letters were so long that the APO sent them back for postage because they were so heavy. Ordinarily we could just write FREE in the upper-right-hand corner, but he had to go to the post office itself to mail his. Strange, very strange. We always thought he had a rather odd relationship with his sister. Especially after we returned to Cam Ranh Bay, when he read us part of one of those letters, in which he included descriptions of his encounters with hookers in graphic detail—like I said, he was an odd guy.

This guy stayed in the same hotel, went on the same tours, and went to the same parties as us. I still can't figure why we didn't tell him to get the hell away from us, but we didn't, so what can I say.

Aside from Von Dran and that things were so expensive, the only bad thing about the trip was the weather—it was freezing. And since none of us had much in the line of civilian clothes, including jackets, we froze the whole time. But we had a great time and enjoyed ourselves in Japan.

TRUCKS

To get anywhere around Cam Ranh Bay, we always rode in trucks, usually two-and-a-half ton trucks, known as "deuce-and-a-halfs." (Anytime there was two of anything in the service, it was called a deuce.) The deuce-and-a-halfs had seats that folded down, but the trucks were really built to haul cargo, not people. So, consequently, the ride was so rough it would give you a literal pain in the side: "short-timer pains." The same pains you might get while running. The best place to ride was standing up behind the cab; that's where the ride was the softest, if that word can be used. God forbid the truck driver found out that someone riding in the back had gotten his shot for the clap; he would hit every hole in the road, just to make the guy's butt hurt worse. Did I ever mention that GIs could be a sadistic bunch?

It was always best to hang on tight when riding in back, because if the truck hit a bump, there was a good possibility you'd get hurt or even bounced right out of the truck. This almost happened to me and another GI one night. When we were responding to a red alert, the driver hit a dip in the road, and if it weren't for the strap that went across the back of the truck, we would both have been flung out onto the road. As it was, my partner's heavy steel pot bounced off, never to be seen again.

Once I was riding in the back of a deuce and a half, and being the sleep-deprived person I was, I fell asleep lying on one of the fold-down bench seats. When the truck went around a corner, I woke to find myself hanging out of the back. I managed to pull myself back in, but I stood up for the rest of the ride. When we reached our destination, I mentioned what had happened to the driver; he had been unaware of my predicament. It proved what could happen with just the slightest bit of inattention. I never fell asleep in the back of a truck again, that's for sure.

The area around Cam Ranh Bay was all sand, no real soil. The sand down at the beach was so fine it squeaked when walked on, like freshly fallen snow. Even though our trucks had six-wheel drive and two-speed transfer cases, they would get stuck in the stuff. Sometimes the trucks would start to hop up and down, due to losing traction in the sand. I have seen the rear wheels of a truck that weighed in the tons hop a foot off the ground. Everyone had to bail when this started to happen. However, for all its shortcomings as a passenger vehicle, the deuce and a half was a great truck and served as the workhorse of the Army in Vietnam.

One of the really weird things to watch in Vietnam was a convoy of trucks going through a village. How it went depended on whose convoy it was: the U.S. Army's, the Vietnamese Army's, or the Koreans'.

Around Cam Ranh Bay, when a convoy of GIs went through a town, the villagers would all run to the side of the road, hoping the GIs would throw them cigarettes or candy (if you threw them anything from C-rations, they would throw it back). They knew the GIs would slow down and take care not to run anyone over, so the road would be lined with people, waving and trying to get us to throw them something.

If the convoy was comprised of Vietnamese or Korean trucks, it was the exact opposite. Everyone ran away and no one stayed at the side of the road, because they knew they would be run over if they got in the way. There would be a phalanx of people running away, kind of like the point of a spear. The Koreans and the Vietnamese just put their right feet on the gas and their left hands on the horn. If you got in the way, that was your tough luck, because they did not slow down for anybody or anything.

The major problem with Army trucks—or any Army vehicles—was that just about any accident was basically not survivable for the occupants. With no seat belts, and wood struts holding up the canvas tops, if they crashed, you were screwed.

One question they would ask when men took an Army driving test was, "If you are driving a truck with a load of GIs in the back, and a little girl runs out in front of you, what do you do?" Of course, the correct answer was, "Kill the little girl." If you tried to make an evasive maneuver, then everyone in back could be killed, so it was one little girl or twenty men. I suppose it depended on who you were asking: GIs or her parents.

On one trip to Nha Trang, we passed the spot where a driver had somehow rolled a deuce and a half off the road. We came upon the crash just as the medevac chopper was leaving. Oddly, while they were used in Vietnam, it was years before medevacs caught on in the States.

FUNNY MONEY

Real money, greenbacks and change, was not allowed in Vietnam. It was a court martial offense to be caught with U.S. currency. Instead, we had MPC (Military Payment Certificates). These came in twenties, tens, fives, and ones, and the change was also in paper, coming in fifty, twenty-five, ten, and five cent increments. It was normal to have a wad of money that would've choked a horse, but which was worth less than ten dollars. Actually, it was kind of cool-looking money, all different colors, with pictures of tanks and airplanes on the bills.

In order to curb the black market and keep MPC out of the hands of the Vietnamese, the style of the bills was changed every once in a while. We would get up one morning and the whole post would be shut down; actually the whole country would be shut down. Then we would line up and exchange our money for the new issue of MPC. This new issue made the old money absolutely worthless, so you didn't want to forget a secret stash.

Of course, this switch would outrage the Vietnamese citizens, who had stashes of illegal MPC. Even though it was illegal for them to poses any kind of U.S. currency, they still did. And whenever there was a changeover, there were howls from the locals. Their secret stashes suddenly weren't worth a red cent, and they were most un-happy.

I had my housegirl buy some blouses for my mom and sister. I paid her for them with MPC, and then forgot the whole thing. Well, my housegirl did not spend the money, but kept it, and of course lost everything when a changeover happened. She came to me and wanted me to pay her for the blouses again. Of course I refused, stating that I had already paid for them and it wasn't my fault she lost out on her end of the deal. After days of her whining, I finally gave her some money back, but never did pay her in full a second time. I just couldn't see paying for something twice, no matter who lost out.

MORE ON DOGS

The dogs the MPs used in the storage areas were a wild card; you never knew what they would do. Fact is, the men I served on guard with were afraid of them—including me.

One night, not too long after we arrived at the bunker in Yankee Area for guard, the MPs had not shown up yet and it was not quite dark, so we were enjoying our last cigarettes for the night.

All of a sudden, I heard a truck grinding up the ravine to the bunker. I looked at the partner on guard and asked, "Who's coming?" and he said, "Oh, that's the MPs coming on duty." The closer the truck got to us, the weirder it was—it sounded like a rolling dog fight. All I could hear was the sound of dogs snarling and growling; they even drowned out the noise of the truck engine. When the truck finally got to the bunker, I observed six MPs and their dogs sitting in the back of a three-quarter-ton truck, and even though the dogs were wearing muzzles, they were carrying on the loudest dogfight I ever heard. It would have been kind of funny if the darn dogs weren't so vicious. I think even the MPs were afraid of them half the time.

One night, one of the dogs somehow got loose and crawled into the bunker through one of the firing ports; everyone cleared out of the bunker, including the MPs. Maybe the dog just wanted out of the rain, but I did not hang around to find out.

Another time, a friend of mine was on guard, and one of the dogs jumped on the bunker and grabbed the sandwiches he had brought along. Rather than saying anything, my friend just let the dog have everything.

The MPs were always trying to get us to pet those dogs, and even though I like dogs, I refused to even try to get friendly with them. I just did not trust them. Looking back on it, I feel sorry for the dogs, but it was a bad time for everyone, dogs included.

Fortunately, the killer guard dogs were not the only representatives of the canine clan around us. We had our own dogs: Charlie, Sam, and Skinny. Charlie and Sam were the company dogs, already there when I first arrived at Cam Ranh. They didn't belong to any one person and alternated between the 174th and the 606th Ordnance

Company. I assume they must have been fed out of the mess hall. But we gave them snacks if we had a care package from home.

Charlie was your typical Southeast Asian dog: light brown, about sixteen inches tall at the shoulder, with a curled tail and probably about fifty pounds. The older of the two, Sam looked like a black and tan coon hound. For some reason, Charlie did not like the Vietnamese and would chase them if he had a chance. He once got ten days in quarantine for biting a housegirl on the butt. But those dogs were good company, and it was fun to have them around the area.

Some of the Vietnamese people who worked for the battalion gave us a dog out at the box shop, and since he was such a skinny little thing, that became his name: Skinny. He was black and white and just your typical puppy, full of energy all the time. We kept him out at the shop and took food out there for him. He must have been pretty lonely out there at night, because there was no guard, and we did not work night shifts unless it was an emergency.

Right after we got Skinny, one of our truck drivers received a Dear John letter from his girlfriend and went on a three-day drinking binge. He and his shotgun stopped by the shop and we all had a snort of Jack Daniels. Eventually, someone had the great idea of giving some to the dog, at first with a little Coke in it, and later just straight booze. That little pup got so drunk. I could not believe that he would drink straight whiskey, but he did. We laughed so hard we almost made ourselves sick, watching that silly dog try to walk. Finally, he passed out, and we put him in his bed.

Was the whole episode cruel? Oh yes, probably borderline animal cruelty, but given the circumstances and the times, I can forgive all of us. It didn't seem to hurt the dog a bit; the next day he was as good as new. No worse for wear as far as we could see, actually. I'm a little surprised it did not kill him, but Skinny came out of it better than the truck driver, who drank so much straight whiskey he lost his voice for a week.

Three

Ready Reaction Force

ALERTS, ALERTS, ALERTS

Alpha Ammunition Storage Area, 1969

Rifle shots cracked, breaking the silence and scaring the daylights out of everyone. Minutes earlier, Colonel Powell, the battalion commander, had hollered, "Get off the truck! There might be incoming!" Since we were parked right in front of a whole pad of 105 mm ammunition, we hustled off the truck—although, if there had really been incoming and the ammunition exploded, the lot of us would still have been blown to bits—and I mean really small bits.

We strung out along the top of large dune, and all I we could see in front of us was the deep ravine, a sand canyon that opened up on to the South China Sea. Colonel Powell told the three men closest to him to fire four shots apiece, trying to get whoever was out there to give themselves away by returning our fire. But either no one was there or they were declining the invitation, because nothing happened. I was a little surprised that the whole damn detachment did not open fire. I never knew we had the discipline to hold our fire.

While we were waiting, a GI asked me, "Hey, how much ammo do you have?"

I told him, "Four magazines. Why?"

It turned out that in all the excitement he had only grabbed one cartridge, so I gave him one or two of mine. I can't believe he only had one bullet. We ended up not seeing anything or anyone, but it was a serious alert because the battalion commander was out with us and that was very unusual. That was also the only time shots were fired, of all the alerts I was on during my year in Vietnam.

I wish I kept count of all the alerts I went on during that year. It must have been a hundred, maybe more. Sometimes it seemed like we spent every night tearing around in a deuce and a half to one storage area or another; the 174th Ordnance Detachment was the battalion's Ready Reaction Force, and we were called out first if an alert was called. If we stayed out most of the night on an alert, we were rewarded by having morning formation at 0700 hours instead of 0630 hours before going to work.

My introduction to alerts in Vietnam did not get off to a very auspicious start. Not too long after I joined the detachment, maybe two weeks in, the battalion called a yellow alert. Now, a yellow alert was kind of a get ready to go sort of thing; we just had to hang loose in case we were needed.

Unfortunately, however, the alert happened to coincide with the opening of the EM Club in Cam Ranh Bay, and most of the detachment was so drunk, I don't think it could have fought a bunch of housegirls and come out the winner. While Mr. Mello was telling us what was going on, someone in back row of the formation barfed his guts out, and everyone started laughing. Good thing it never went beyond yellow alert, because we were a pretty useless bunch that night.

But humor aside, alerts were serious business; the ammunition we carried was real and a war was going on, and we never knew when the war might come to us. Though we didn't end up seeing anyone, there must have been someone out there at least one of those times—I can't imagine we were out there by ourselves and that nothing caused the alert every time. More than a few times, I was sent back to the company area to load the entire basic load of rifle ammunition (fifteen thousand rounds) and bring it back our alert station.

When a red alert was called, we would get our weapons and ammunition from the arms room, climb aboard a truck, and take off, and then end up sitting in the truck most of the night until we were released to go back. One night, we were parked in Yankee Area at about 0200 hours, sitting there in the dark waiting for something to happen or someone tell us what to do. Since it was dark, we did not know that we had parked right next to the 81mm mortar they used to shoot illumination rounds. In fact, we didn't even know the mortar existed until they dropped a round down the tube with what was apparently a full charge. When that thing went off, it scared the crap out of us. We thought something blew up. Before we had figured out what happened, everyone scrambled off the trucks.

The worst time for alerts was during Tet 1969. It got so we would work all day, go to chow, return to the company area, take a shower if there was water, go to the arms room to get our weapons and sleep with them, and then, in a few hours, go out on an alert for the rest of the night. This went on for weeks. I didn't realize I hadn't written my parents in weeks until I received a letter from my worried mom, asking me what was going on. Everyone slept fully clothed except for boots, so we could be ready to go in a few minutes. But we never saw anything or anyone out there, no matter how much sleep we lost.

One memorable night, we were called out to Yankee Storage Area, and there was really supposed to be enemy there. We went through the wire and out into the brush, and someone approached me and a guy named Wilson, and told us to go down to bunker number two. Since it was pitch black and we didn't have the slightest idea where the bunker was, we were a little hesitant. But we were told there was a stake in the ground to show us where the bunker was.

Of course, no one knew the stake had been knocked down, so we could not find the darn thing. We wandered around for about twenty minutes or so. We were petrified someone would shoot us and ask for the password later, since we made an awful lot of noise. Finally we quit searching and just sat in the brush up above the road for the rest of the night. We could see the road, so we kind of did our job, but we never did find the stupid bunker.

That same night, my good friend, sergeant Ken Nowitzky, came within a microsecond of getting shot by a very nervous GI before the GI recognized him. Sergeant Nowitzky had been checking on the men, and he appeared very suddenly and then could not remember the password. Everyone was on edge that night because there were really supposed to be some VC out there, but we saw no one.

We may have been ordnance men, but it seemed we spent an awful lot of time trying to be infantry. Yet, as I said, we never saw anything. Maybe just by being there, we stopped the storage areas from being attacked. I hope we managed to do some good with all that running around in the middle of the night, even if we never fired our weapons.

Four

Work Places

STORAGE AREAS

Unlike many major bases around Vietnam, Can Ranh Bay did not have many amenities handy (except safety, which was a good thing). But if there was one thing we had enough of in Cam Ranh, it was ammunition. Whatever caliber—millimeter, inch—we had it a million times over. Driving through Yankee Area, it was amazing to see all the ammo stacked up. It was stacked in pads, each about seventy-five by fifty feet, surrounded by a berm about fifteen feet high. The berm was not there for looks; it was meant to contain a blast if the pad of ammo blew up. I wonder how much one of the pads of, let's say, eight inch rounds would weigh, and how many rounds of M16 ammo one pad held. Each storage area must have had fifty pads, and there were three storage areas in our battalion, so you can see we had plenty of the stuff. My detachment worked on one lot of 7.62 mm minigun ammunition. That was 2.5 million rounds, and that was just one lot!

Most ammunition moved out of Cam Ranh by truck convoy. These left pretty much every day, so the areas were always busy and in constant movement. The trucks would be loaded with pallets of ammo and the loads tied down. It was interesting to watch the convoys form up. The gun trucks were my favorites to watch. They were armored and usually had two M60 machine guns per side with a fifty cal. over the cab and several men with M79 grenade launchers in the back. Those trucks were formidable weapons.

I heard that if a particular truck driver was a real ass, then he might end up with C4 explosives and blasting caps on his truck when the convoy was loaded. Now, this is a real no-brainer for anyone familiar with loading trucks with ammo, but blasting caps are rather touchy and could detonate the C4. Scratch one truck driver and truck if that happened. I didn't see this happen, but I have little doubt that it did.

Being around thousands of tons of explosives was a bit surreal. I mean, it was incredibly dangerous, but after a while, it seemed like no big thing. U.S. ammunition was pretty safe, but you couldn't be too stupid around it.

The only time I was ever really concerned was in Yankee Area, in a pad known as Pad 501. You could probably call it an "ammo dump." Every kind of ammo lay strewn around: single rounds, multiples of some ordnance, some contained, some not. Turning my head and talking to someone, I tripped over some 81 mm mortar rounds rolling around in the dust. How they got out of their containers is beyond me, but there they were. That pad was the only location where I did not feel safe working, even if I was being careful. The problem with high explosives is that if one blows up, then they all blow up—sympathetic detonation. So it does not really matter how careful one person was; everyone had to be on the same page as far as safety went, or everyone could die.

The day before, while we had been looking for Pad 501, we were in the wrong area. We were looking in Alpha Area. There, we ran across projectiles for the sixteen-inch guns on the USS *Missouri*. Now, those were some impressive projectiles. They were about five feet long and weighed a ton apiece. I think the powder containers weighed something like four hundred pounds each. I couldn't imagine being around one of those when it detonated.

We worked our tails off in the storage areas. I spoke to a Lieutenant Angel from the 611th while we were paying the Vietnamese laborers at the CMO (Civilian Management Office), and he said he was amazed at the work the men in his company did. He said the company was at sixty percent strength and they did one hundred forty percent of the assigned workload.

BRASS YARD

The brass yard and related box shop were basically just recycling operations on a very large scale. And instead of cans and plastic bottles, we dealt with instruments of death and destruction. They were reconditioned stateside and reloaded and sent back to be used again. Just recycling, with a different slant.

In our brass yard, both small arms brass and things like 105 mm howitzer cases were sent to us. The small arms brass used to arrive in large metal containers called conexes; inside each was a slip of paper signed by some unknown second lieutenant stating that, after inspection, this container contained no live ammunition. Accompanying this declaration would be hand grenades, hundreds of rounds of live small arms ammunition, Claymore mines, and blasting caps, both electric and with fuses. We never knew what would tumble out. I thought that these little presents were included on purpose, just to show us REMFs (Rear Echelon Mother Fucker) what was really going on in the war. I was always amazed none of this ordnance exploded, especially the electric blasting caps, which tended to be kind of touchy.

Most of our work force consisted of women, young and old. There were very few men, and those we did have were middle-aged, too old to be drafted. One memorable day, a Vietnamese *mamasan* named Uk took an electric blasting cap and pantomimed how to hook it up to a blasting machine and set off the a charge—a somewhat disconcerting demonstration for those of us present. One can only guess where she learned this skill.

Of course, all of our sorting was done under the supervision of a GI who removed the live rounds. All live rounds and other ordnance were put in a bunker to be dealt with by EOD (Explosive Ordnance Demolition); in other words, they blew it up. I imagine some of the Vietnamese must have been under pressure to steal the live ammo. I never caught them at it, nor did anyone else there—but I am sure it happened.

At one time, brass, especially the 105 mm, was delivered in trucks pulling gondola-like trailers, according to Sergeant Nowitsky. These would sometimes come directly from the forward fire bases, and assorted body parts would be included with the artillery brass. He never said exactly which particular parts were the most common. I expect they were given a summary burial in the sands of Cam Ranh Bay; hopefully no one out there is missing a part that was buried in some unknown spot by the GIs of the 174th Ordnance Detachment.

Sergeant Nowitsky was one of the real movers and shakers of the 174th Ordnance Detachment. He was in at the start of the brass yard and developed a lot of the recycling programs there. He also started the civilian management office—he was in charge when I took over, and he was the one who recommended me for the job. He had extended his tour by six months to quality for an early discharge out of the Army, so he spent eighteen months in Vietnam. He was the go-to sergeant in the company.

Outside my office at the CMO.

Sergeant Keenan always clenched his cigarettes between his teeth, instead of holding them between his lips like the rest of us. After Sergeant Nowitsky rotated home, the brass yard was under his supervision. One day, we were coming back from chow and we found Sergeant Keenan just fit to be tied. I had never seen him so pissed off. It turned out that when he came back to the brass yard, he found a couple of the *babysans* (young Vietnamese girls) taking a bath in our water trailer.

Now, this trailer held five hundreds gallons, which may not sound like much to some people, but in Vietnam, five hundred gallons of fresh water was not easy to come by. The whole thing had to be drained out into the sand after being contaminated by those two girls.

★★★★

One day, a truck came into the yard with a load of five-inch-rocket containers, aluminum tubes about three feet long—and for some reason, a couple of them still contained the warheads. During transit, the warheads had come out of the containers and were bouncing around in the back of the truck. Since they were not fused, there was no real danger, but the truck driver was really frightened when he saw them. The whole crew had a good laugh at the poor driver's expense.

RENOVATION LINE

Our job at the renovation line was to make sure that the ammunition did what it was supposed to do; that is, fly straight and blow up without jamming the guns. In other words, we had to make sure the ammunition killed people. If we did our job correctly, our side lived and the other side died—simple as that.

The 174th Ordnance Detachment had a number functions and duties, but the renovation line was our main job, and that was where a majority of the men worked, day in and day out. We worked on every type of ammunition the Army had, from 7.62 rounds all the way up to 8 inch and 175 mm artillery, and everything in between, from mines to mortars.

The renovation line was, by necessity, located away from any populated or storage areas, since by definition, there was something wrong with the ammunition we dealt with. We literally had tons of ammunition stacked around most of the time. It was actually a really

A very rare photo of the Renovation Line. (Courtesy of Joe Linsner)

nice location, right down on the South China Sea. The sand was so fine and clean, it squeaked like freshly fallen snow when walked on, and was as white as the snow, too. The ocean was crystal clear, and the waves were small most of the time, though the depth of the water dropped off fast.

The ammunition we worked on was delivered to us from the storage areas. If the boxes had been in storage for awhile, then we often received more than just ammunition in them. The boxes made fine living quarters for snakes and rats, and ants especially loved them, so we always kept cans of insecticide and a shovel handy to deal with the squatters.

One of the worst batches of ammo we ever worked on was a batch of 105 mm smoke ammunition. Believe it or not, the ammunition had been made in 1943, and it looked it. It was odd, working on something that was made when my father was in the service during World War II. I don't know where this batch of ammo had been stored, but it was in such bad shape that most of it was thrown away. All 105 mm ammunition comes in a heavy cardboard containers with the projectile at one end and the case at the other. A good share of this ammo had been wet so long it was impossible to get it out of the container. The cardboard was stuck to the projectile. Any rounds like this were discarded, since we had no new containers. We had a machine that pulled the containers apart so we would not have do it by hand, and even it couldn't pull this stuff apart.

****

Several men managed to be banished from the renovation line and the storage areas. One, who had absolutely no fear of the ammunition, I mentioned in a previous chapter. He was caught trying to juggle 40 mm rounds while standing in the midst of thousands of rounds. While U.S. ammunition is really safe, and probably nothing would have happened, he was never allowed back at the line or in the storage areas again for obvious reasons. Anyone who would try that couldn't be allowed or trusted around the ammo.

Another man was kicked out of both areas for the opposite reason: he was scared to death of handling any ammunition. He would visibly shake if he had his hands on any kind of explosive, so he was banished from the renovation line to the company area. I don't quite know what he did for the rest of his tour, but he did not handle any ammunition again, that's for sure. Lives depended on how people acted or reacted while handling ammunition. One mistake and a lot of men would have been killed. There were no second chances.

Five

Guard Duty

FIRST TIME ON GUARD

After I had been in-country for a couple of weeks or so, I saw my name on the roster for guard duty at the renovation line, along with Danny Payton's. So, at the appointed time, I drew my weapon and climbed aboard a truck for the ride out to the reno line.

Now, because of the renovation line's isolated location on Cam Ranh Bay, standing guard duty out there turned out to be very lonely. It was right down on the beach and the bunker for guard duty was on top of a sand dune behind our break shack. When you were on top of the bunker, the whole beach was easily visible. To the front, the South China Sea went on forever, and to the north and south you could see miles of beach. There was no radio at the reno line, only a field phone at the break shack; if the phone rang, I had to climb down off the bunker and down the sand dune to answer it; a clumsy arrangement if I ever saw one. In an actual attack, I would have had to climb down among the attackers to call for help.

The usual format for guard was two hours on and two hours off. I had first shift, from dark until about 2200 hours. And then midnight till 0200, and 0400 until dawn. The first two hours were OK, and then I woke my guard partner, Payton, for relief, and he took over until approximately midnight. This second shift was really the worst: it was raining, very dark and windy, and I could see absolutely nothing. All I could hear was the breakers crashing ashore on the beach; someone could have been shouting, and I would not have heard a thing.

So I sat there in the rain, watching water drip off the muzzle of my rifle, wondering, *What the hell am I doing out here?* There I was, the Army's version of the canary in a coal mine—with no miners around—waiting for something happen, wondering how I was going to survive the next eleven months in this asylum. I sat there, scared, extremely lonely, rehearsing in my mind what I would do if I saw anyone on the beach. But after two hours, I was just lonely, scared, and wet. My next shift would be from 0400 hours until 0600, and that would prove to be somewhat more eventful.

At around 0400 hours, I was back, sitting there in the dark, but at least it had quit raining. Sometime after sunup along came a sampan, sailing approximately four hundred fifty meters off the beach, parallel to it, heading south. Getting down on the top of the bunker, I put my sights on it and got ready to fire—I was a very good shot with an M14. But our instructions were so vague, I didn't know if I should fire or not, and at that range, I could've ruined the day of whomever was sailing the sampan. Visions of a court-martial appeared before me, so I let him go, watching him sail out of sight. Later, I told the first sergeant about the incident, and he said it was probably a good thing that I did not fire. It wouldn't have been good to kill an innocent Vietnamese.

Not long after the sampan incident, the crew showed up to start work at the renovation line for the day, and we got a ride back to the company area. I served on guard many more times after that, but I always made sure I did my time at the bunker in Yankee Ammunition Storage Area, where we had a radio and it was not so isolated. If I had ever encountered enemy at the renovation line, by the time I was sure of that and got anyone to come help, it would have been too late for me.

PASSWORD

You might not think there would be a downside to not being attacked. While I was in Vietnam, we were lucky in that our ammunition storage areas never were. While that was positive, it also meant guard duty could be boring and tedious, and people could get careless. And being careless in a combat zone usually has tragic results.

Many different companies had responsibility for various bunkers in the storage areas. One of the bunkers in Yankee Area was manned by a supply company. The way the bunkers were constructed made it impossible to stand guard inside of them—you couldn't see much from inside—so most people sat on top of them while on guard. Doing so was also cooler. Whoever was off-duty might sleep in the bunker if he could stand the smell and the heat. If it was really hot, he might just sleep on top. If it was raining, the guard would put on his poncho and sit in the rain. If, by any chance, whoever was on guard had to leave his post for any reason, such as a nature call, then he was to wake up the off-duty guard and tell him he was leaving. He could not just walk away.

One particular night, two men were on guard. One had been in-country quite a while and the other was brand new—it was his first time on guard. Apparently, however, they had become good friends in a short time.

Now, when someone was brand new in Vietnam and hadn't ever been on guard before, they were usually scared to death (I was). So this was our scenario: we had one man who was scared and another who was just bored. The scared guy was sleeping and the old bored guy was on guard.

As it happened the bored guy had to pee and walked out to the wire to obey his call of nature—neglecting to wake up his scared friend and tell him what was going on. In the meantime, the scared guy woke up. Looking out the firing port, he saw someone walking toward the bunker and grabbed his rifle.

Here he also failed to follow procedure; he should have hollered out the password and waited for the countersign. Instead, he just opened fire. Unfortunately, he must have paid a lot of attention during basic training, because he shot his friend seven times. Now, a 7.62 mm round at almost point-blank range is devastating, and that is exactly what struck the bored guy.

Who was to blame for this tragedy? The men involved, the war, the people who started the war? Perhaps it's useless to place blame. The outcome was one dead man and another scarred for life. The man who did the shooting went into such deep shock that he had to be hospitalized.

This was another of those casualties that got the label "non-combat-related death." I always laugh when I see that phrase; if it wasn't for combat, what were we doing there? It makes it sound like whoever was killed was not quite as dead or something, but I am sure the relatives miss them just as much, I mean since dead is dead—no matter how a person got that way.

That last point is an important one. When I first went to Vietnam, I was worried about being killed or wounded by the enemy, VC or NVA. After I was there for a time, I became aware that everyone was the enemy as far as going home was concerned. If I wanted to go home, then I had better pay attention to what was going on around me, and there were still some obvious slip ups as you can see. Does it matter who shoots you? Kills you in a truck accident or stabs you? The only difference is that you don't get a Purple Heart for "non-combat-related death." Don't you love that phrase?

IS ANYONE OUT THERE?
Yankee Ammunition Storage Area, 1969

I was on guard duty, sometime after dark in the pouring rain. I was talking to an MP (we shared a bunker with them); he was telling me about their dogs that were designed to kill.

While we were BSing, one of the dogs attacked the other MP. I heard the jaws slam shut. I thought, *Just what we need, killer dogs that don't care who they kill.* Grabbing the dog, the handler hooked the leash onto the dog's choke chain collar, stepped out of the bunker into the downpour, and began to swing the dog around and around on the leash. I thought it was kind of an odd way to discipline a dog.

Finally, the dog passed out, and the handler threw him down in the muck and walked back into the bunker out of the rain. I asked him, "You going to leave him there?"

The handler said, "Yeah, he'll be all right."

I watched the dog, lying in the rain, and felt nothing. Pretty soon, the dog was low crawling, back toward the bunker, apparently recovered from his near-death experience, and the dog and the MP were buddies again. I wondered, *If that dog killed me, would they still buddies?* They said the NVA especially hated being killed by dogs (because of their religious significance), and I thought we may have had something in common: a nightmare about being killed by a dog. I sat there on a sandbag, thinking, *Damn, I hate this place.*

Later on the MPs and their killer dogs were out looking for something else to kill, besides me and each other. My guard partner was sleeping, so it was just me and my corner of the war, just me and my M14, looking at nothing, seeing nothing. The radio, which was our link to help, crackled to life. We reported in every hour with "situation negative," though positive reports could be called in anytime.

Suddenly, a voice came out of the darkness, a harsh metallic tone: "81 Alfa Zulu, this is 41 Tango Charlie, over." Then silence, nothing more. Since that wasn't me, I paid no attention and went back to looking at nothing. Again, the voice said, "81 Alfa Zulu, this is 41 Tango Charlie." Of course he was trying to give his "situation negative" report, but all he got was silence and me.

Again he tried and again he failed. His link to the light was severed, and he was alone in the Southeast Asian night. He tried for the fourth time and again he failed, but I thought, *Son of a bitch, did his voice just go up in pitch?* I was interested now—was it possible someone was more afraid of this place than me? Again he tried, but his only reward was silence. I kept expecting him to break his sound barrier, but all he got was fear and me. He tried another time and it sounded like his fear was reducing him to tears. Vietnam at night was a very forbidding place.

He finally screamed into the mike, "Can anyone out there hear me"? That was my cue; I picked up the radio and said, "41 Tango Charlie, this is 41 Alfa Tango. Can I be of assistance?" He was no longer alone; he had me.

I asked if he wanted me to report in for him, and he said "Yes, yes, yes." I called 81 Alfa Zulu and reported his situation negative (was this a lie?) and the bored lieutenant said, "Roger that." So we both went back to being in the darkness, to negative reports, snarling dogs, and drenching rain. Does he remember me like I remember him, I wonder?

The hours always passed slowly while I was on guard, and I found it hard to stay awake. Rain continued to confine us to the bunker, which had started to smell stale, of tobacco, sweat, urine, dirt, and wet dogs. I knew the night was almost over when I could hear the truck coming up the ravine to pick us up. I thought, *How many days do I have left?*

Years later, I told his story to a number of people, and their response was invariably, "Why didn't you respond earlier? It was obvious the man was scared out of his wits, and you just let him dangle!"

I suppose, in hindsight, I should have responded earlier, but to be honest, it never occurred to me. I just assumed he would get through to give his situation report. But in my defense, there is the real possibility that many other guards heard him and did not respond, and just said, "Fuck him," under their breath. So at least I responded, although a tad bit late.

"PUT IT OUT YOURSELF"

Once again while on guard duty at Yankee Ammunition Storage Area, I found myself talking to the MPs about their killer dogs. I never saw those MPs in the light of day. They always seemed to come by in the dark, kind of like the VC were supposed to. The only time I actually saw their faces was in the light from flares, which was useless in terms of aiding recognition, so describing them would be kind of like trying to describe someone after seeing his shadow. They were anonymous figures, as were their dogs.

Once, one of those MPs told me he was thinking about buying his dog and taking him home after his tour, which the Army allowed. I was more than a little dubious about this plan. I wasn't sure you could deprogram a dog; once a killer, always a killer, as far as I was concerned.

On that particular night, the MPs were telling me the dogs would only alert on another human being, not wild animals or anything else, so if a dog alerted, then they were sure someone was in the brush. I assumed that was why they viewed the whole area as a free-fire zone. If the dogs alerted, they could shoot. We, on the other hand, theoretically were supposed to get permission over the radio, but since no one was allowed or supposed to be out there, I always figured I would shoot first and radio later.

The main bunker was the one at the head of a large ravine; it was situated right next to the wire and three roads that came out at the bunker. The MPs patrolled all of them. When we finished talking, the MPs took off down one of the roads on patrol. They had not gone more than fifty feet when one of the dogs alerted, and started barking and snarling like crazy. Instantly it went from another boring night on guard to absolute chaos: the dogs were barking and the MPs were screaming for a flare while trying to control the dogs and aim their rifles.

I ran to the bunker for a flare, and my partner locked and loaded his rifle. I remember thinking, I guess I'll find out what the shooting war is all about, as I fumbled in the box for a flare. The flare we used, Lima 312, was about the size of a paper towel roll. To use it, you'd pull off one end and fit it to the opposite end. You'd strike it with the other hand, and this launched the flare. As always, I made sure the flare was not a red one, as red flares meant enemy contact and would cause an instant alert. Stepping out of the bunker, I fired it skyward, and then, taking my rifle, ran down to where the dogs were barking. When the flare burst overhead, we were all bathed in that weird, almost metallic light.

Despite what the dogs were telling us, we could see nothing, and they quit barking soon afterward. We received a call on the radio from the officer on duty, who asked about the flare. I explained we had a dog alert on something, but that we saw nothing. He said, "OK, but keep me posted if anything else happens."

I said, "Don't worry." In ten minutes, it was back to being another boring night on guard. I always wondered what those goofy dogs hit on.

Later on that night, the same two MPs were back at the bunker, and for some reason one of them decided to shoot a flare—the reason why is lost to time. Anyway, instead of going straight up, the flare went horizontal, flying across a ravine and hitting the ground. The rocket stopped burning, the parachute deployed with a pop, and the flare burst in the brush, starting a fire. I thought, *Oh wonderful, now we'll have a forest fire on our hands*, as the fire crackled and popped in the background.

We stood there, watching the fire burn, looking at the MP, who wore an "it was an accident" expression. I asked in my most sarcastic voice, "How in the hell did that happen?"

About that time, we heard our radio. One of tower guards must have seen the fire and reported it. Anyway, some officer, who sounded kind of pissed, wanted to know what happened.

I said, "Well, we had a rather horizontal flare, and it started a fire."

His only response: "Go put it out." End of transmission.

I told the MP who fired the darn thing what the officer said, and he had the nerve to ask for help in the putting the fire out. I looked him and said, "You started it; you put it out." There was no way I was going out there in the middle of the night to wander around in the brush and try to put out a fire. I had been in Vietnam much too long for such foolishness. I was well into the tenth month of my tour at this time—much longer than the MPs or my guard partner. Time in country counted for something, as far as I was concerned, and someone had to watch the radio in case something happened to them.

My partner on guard said he would go with them, so the three of them went through the wire and stomped the fire out, while I stood watch and kept the radio company. After a while they came back and I reported in that the fire was out. Those MPs were pissed at me for not helping and said so, but all I said was, "Try shooting them up in the air next time." Needless to say, we were not buddies after that.

✷✷✷✷

As I have said, not being able to see well was one of the scarier aspects of guard duty. If you stare at an object too long, it will appear to move; thus, it was very difficult to decide if someone was really out there or not, and what might need to be done. If there was no moon, then it was impossible to see anything.

The starlight scope was invented to harness the light from the stars or moon in order to enable you to see at night. I personally could not see very well through the darn things. Objects viewed though a starlight scope looked like really bad color TV pictures—the image was green and the objects viewed looked kind of black. I could only make things out if I already knew what I was looking at beforehand.

One night on guard we were given a starlight scope to use, with, as usual, no real training on how to use it. Two MPs were helping us play with it when, up on the ridge, a trip flare went off in the perimeter wire. Using the scope, I looked up at the vicinity of the flare and saw nothing, but something set off the flare, so we kept at it.

One of the MPs said he saw some kind of cat, and that's what he thought set off the flare. My partner on guard said he saw it too. I had to take their word for it, because I just could not see anything. Since no one was shooting and nothing blew up, I guess they were right and it was some kind of jungle cat.

****

Guard duty was tedious, boring, and dull, and then could suddenly turn demanding and—once in a while—frightening. It was difficult to stay awake, and to avoid becoming blasé when nothing happened for a long time. If the weather was bad, it could be a miserable experience and a two-hour shift could take forever to end. Most people can only relate to guard duty based on what they have seen in movies or on TV. But TV guards never seem to fall asleep and always walk back and forth devoting their utmost attention to the task. They are never soaking wet, cold, lonely, scared, miserable—and wanting to get the hell out of wherever they are.

6TH CC

Just another boring night on guard at Yankee Storage Area—or maybe hot and sweaty and boring might be a better description. Nothing going on; even the MPs and their killer dogs weren't around. Nothing to do except stare at the darkness on my shift, and catch a little sleep on top of the bunker during my two hours off.

Sometime during the night, during my shift, I heard explosions off to the north. As this was happening, I woke up my partner and said, "That does not sound good," and he agreed. As the explosions continued, we were filled with anxiety, but we decided that they must be up at the Air Force base. Both of us figured they could be rockets or mortars exploding. Neither of us could have guessed it was a sapper attack, and the explosions were satchel charges being thrown into barracks.

The radio came to life, and we were informed that there was an attack in progress. They told us to be extra vigilant because the powers that be thought the enemy could be creating a diversion while the ammunition storage areas were attacked. That did not give us a warm and fuzzy feeling, I can tell you. Anyway, they called an alert and our whole company ended up in the storage area with us for the rest of the night.

It turned out that the NVA (or the VC) had attacked the 6th CC, a hospital next to the Air Force base. It was not done as any kind of ruse; they attacked the hospital because they wanted to. Why they would attack a place full of wounded is beyond me. But they got in— apparently there were no guards on duty—and threw satchel charges into as many barracks as they could, and then got away without suffering any casualties themselves.

It gave us a helpless feeling to have been sitting there listening to the explosions, and then later find out what was really going on. There was nothing we could have done, since we were miles away, but still, it did give us an odd feeling.

AND WHAT WAS I DOING THERE?

Six

Local Nationals

THE VIETNAMESE

Of all the goddamn days to miss work; they have to be sick or whatever on payday. Good grief, what a total pain in the butt. That was what was running through my mind while I was riding in a truck, taking a load of Vietnamese workers who had missed payday to the finance office at Cam Ranh. I knew I'd be spending the better part of a day waiting for them, since I couldn't leave them there alone, wandering around the main post, looking for a ride home. While I was in charge of the CMO, doing this became sort of a ritual after every payday.

On this particular day, as I was sitting there waiting for the laborers, along came a guy I went to high school with, Richard Sotelo. *Of all the places to run into someone from home!* I can't remember what he was doing there in the finance office.

I do not think any of the Vietnamese employees were trying anything illegal, like getting paid twice. I recognized most of the men who worked for me, and I had sat there the day before when everyone else got paid. Ghost employees were a problem in Vietnam, people on the payroll who did not work and split their pay with someone above them.

Until I took over the CMO, I was not that familiar with the Vietnamese. We had housegirls in the barracks, and there were always whores running around the company area at night, and of course I worked with them in the brass yard. But I never got to know them for who they were, and really had no respect for them as a people. Maybe part of that was because of training; it's hard to kill someone you respect and like.

✳✳✳✳

Leaving Vietnam left a great empty space in my life and in my heart. My housegirl, Mai, has haunted me for years—I really liked her as person, and a friend, although it took me some time to realize it. I think I didn't treat her very well when I left. I just wanted to get out of that place and go home. I don't remember if I even said goodbye; she had been my housegirl for a year, washing my clothes and such things. There was no sex or anything like that involved; we were just friends and I really miss her, and not knowing what happened to her bothers me to this day. It may sound silly, but I always wonder if she isn't right here in California somewhere. It would not surprise me if she were, that is, if she managed to get out of the country after the war.

Like almost all young GIs, I referred to Vietnamese people as "gooks" and never thought about it at all. It was just what was done, that's all, nothing more. I never thought about if they actually minded it or not, and wouldn't have cared if I did. And I probably would've kept my opinions if it weren't for the CMO job, which really did change my understanding of people.

The evolution of my mind began one day with a line of people who had missed payday. I was sitting at my desk, listening to everyone's story through one of my interpreters. Anyway, some *mamasan* was standing in front of me, tearfully telling my why she had missed payday and why she needed the money. It was hot and humid in my little office, and I was not in a good mood. As I sat there listening to her, I was watching a stain on her left breast get larger by the second. She was very pregnant, and I suppose it was milk.

All of the sudden, the thought struck me that it could have been my mom standing in front of me, and that she was obviously going to be someone's mom. The Vietnamese instantly became recognizable as people, and I realized they were just like everyone else, no different, all the same. Why this particular thought took ten months to find me is unknown. Maybe I am a slow learner or something, but at least it hit me. From then on, I never called the Vietnamese gooks or anything else derogatory. Could just have been a growing up sort of thing, I suppose—after all, though I had more responsibility than most people ever have, being in charge of 235 Vietnamese laborers, I was a twenty-one year old spec four.

✳✳✳✳

At the CMO, each day began when the workers were dropped off from the ferry dock; from there, some of them just walked to work at our box shop. Most of the other Vietnamese people would be picked and taken to various places for work. The majority of them worked in our brass yard, where they sorted empty (hopefully) brass for shipment back to the States to be reused.

A couple of times, men from other areas came and asked if they could "borrow" some of the Vietnamese for a day. What they needed was labor for a specific task and were probably under the gun to get it done and didn't have enough help. So normally I obliged them, not for money, but for trade in kind, like new fatigues or socks— things that weren't readily available. The workers liked it, because

Me, hard at work in my office at the CMO.

they got to go someplace new, and for some, it was a new opportunity to steal something if they so desired.

One of the perks that came with being in charge of the CMO was that I had my own secretary, a Vietnamese woman named Kien. She really did very little as a secretary, but she was one of my better interpreters. Her typing skills were dubious, to say the least.

Every two weeks, we had to do the overtime authorizations sheets. These allowed the Vietnamese KPs in our mess halls to work more than the normal forty hours. Since we had no copy machines or anything like that back then, they had to be typed up each time. It was amazing; each time I asked Kien to type up the overtime authorizations, she would give me this blank look, and ask, "What are you talking about?"

I got so pissed at her one day, I told her to get the hell out of her chair, and I would type up the damn things myself. She was amazed that I knew how to type, and I said, "What do you think, you are the only one around the fucking place that knows how to type?" I never did figure out why she played dumb all the time, but the next time I asked her, it was the same crap.

Each authorization had to be signed by the officer from the headquarters company. My last day on the job before I returned home, some stupid lieutenant refused to sign the darn things. No matter how I explained that it didn't mean the people would work that many hours, only that they could, if needed, he still refused. Finally I just walked away, said, "To hell with it," and left the problem to my successor, Spec Five Overmeyer. That job was a real pain in the butt, as far as dealing with the Army bureaucracy went, but it did allow me to really get to know the Vietnamese as a people, and understand them just a bit.

****

One thing I never could understand about the Vietnamese was their habit of chewing betel nuts, one of the vilest habits I have ever seen. None of the younger people did it, mostly just the older generation. Chewing betel nuts turns teeth a dark black, while giving the chewer bright red spit. Once I told a *mamasan* who worked for me that if she spit on me, I was going to shoot her. I wouldn't have, but she got the point—to look before she spit. It was said that underneath the black, their teeth were nice and white, but I never got close enough to a betel nut chewer to find out.

****

Toward the end of my tour of duty, a strip show came to our company area. I can't remember too much about the show, except that my housegirl washed the roll of film I took photos with—scratch one roll of film!

When the show was over and the performers were ready to leave, a staff sergeant came around and asked my friend Herzog if he wanted to ride shotgun for the trip back to Nha Trang. Herzog, being a good guy, said no, because he was engaged and did not want to cheat on his fiancée. This trip would be an overnight; the men would be turned loose in town until the next morning.

I said, "Hey, let me go. I'll ride shotgun." The staff sergeant cleared it with my first sergeant and, after I grabbed my weapon, we took off for Nha Trang. I am surprised they let us go, since it was almost dark, and it was completely dark by the time we got to Nha Trang. When we had turned in our weapons (no weapons were allowed in town), the staff sergeant said the truck driver, Delk, and I were on our own until the next morning. He drove us to a bar, dropped us off, and said, "See you in the morning."

We walked into the bar, and of course quickly became the center of attraction for the bargirls, since we were the only paying customers. But what we wanted was a place to sleep and a girl for the night, and for that we had to negotiate with the *mamasan* of the bar. If memory serves me right, it was twenty bucks for a girl and a bed for the night. Here is where I wish I had just stayed back in Cam Ranh and spent the night in my own bed.

The girl who wanted to go with me looked really young, but since the only lighting was from a string of small Christmas lights, I couldn't tell for sure. I asked, "How old are you?" She said seventeen, and I said that was old enough. It is amazing how you can rationalize things to yourself and have it make sense at the time. I don't know how old she was, but I'm sure she was not seventeen. If it had happened in the States, I would have done time for that night. I knew it was wrong, that she was too young, but I went with her anyway. I can say it was dark, I was young, it was a war, but it still doesn't make things right, and I regret it to this day.

The next morning, Delk and I left. We tried to find our way back downtown, where we were to meet the truck and the staff sergeant—the only problem being that we did not know which way to go. Another one of those "it just disappeared without a trace" instances and "no one knows a thing" situations. Finally we found a main road; figuring it must be Highway 1, we started walking.

A few minutes into our journey, a convoy of trucks loaded with Vietnamese troops went by. No big thing—until they started calling us every dirty name in the book, and flipping us off, and doing everything else they could think of to insult us. We just took it; there were too many of them for it to be wise to holler back. But I can say we weren't amused, and I wondered why we were there, if this was what we received as thanks for coming to their country.

After a long walk, we finally spied landmarks we recognized, and found our way back to the truck and the staff sergeant. On the way back to Cam Ranh Bay, we were stopped at a roadblock by the MPs and had to talk our way out of a speeding ticket. Can you believe it? Speeding in a combat zone!

****

One terrible memory from Cam Ranh was of a night when a number of GIs had sex with a couple of whores, and did not pay them afterward. When I say a number, I actually mean ten or fifteen. I suppose it could be called rape, because there was never any plan to pay them for their services. It was intended as a gang rape from the get-go.

Fifteen years later, I happened to mention this incident to a girlfriend, and she wanted to know if I had turned the men in for rape. I looked at her and said, "Are you kidding me?" I went on to explain that if I had taken it upon myself to do that, there was a very good chance I would have been killed in a fragging or a shooting, and she would have never met me. She didn't believe me; she just could not wrap her mind around the fact that to say anything would have meant my life. I tried to explain, but it was no use; she couldn't understand any of it. No doubt she thought I was a coward for doing nothing.

Maybe I should have put those girls' well-being above my own life, but I had to live with those men. They were not from another town, or across town, or even a different street. They lived within feet of me, and I worked with them every day. If I had done the "right thing," it was a real possibility that one of them or one of their friends would have stabbed me in my sleep, or worse. Remember, this was a combat zone, where everyone had weapons and we worked with explosives day in and day out, and "accidents" happened. It was not black and white. If one of the housegirls were raped, then no problem, I would have stepped up. But I felt less ready to die for a Vietnamese whore who did not get paid. I thought of it as saving my own life, and still do.

✳✳✳✳

One morning, Thom, one of our housegirls, arrived bruised and battered, with road rash on all visible parts of her body, including a large raspberry on her right cheekbone. When I asked about the bruises and road rash, she explained it was from a motorbike crash. Anyone who had spent any time across the bay could readily believe that. When we went across the bay each day, we grew to feel disappointed if we did not see at least one motorbike crash. This being a country where no one had a driver's license, its roads were strictly survival of the fittest—kind of like traffic anarchy.

While discussing the war one night over too much beer and too many cigarettes, a couple of us waxing philosophical came up with a novel solution to the Vietnam War. Our idea was to supply a Honda

Ready for the ride back to Cam Ranh Bay from Nha Trang.

50 motorbike to each and every VC and NVA in the country. We figured that within six months, most of them would be disabled or dead from crashes. Considering how much the war was costing, we figured it would be a bargain for the American taxpayer.

****

I have always thought that the VC cadre across the bay knew exactly who we were in the 174th Ordnance Detachment, and probably in the whole 191st Ordnance Battalion. One time, I was at the barbershop, where all the barbers were young women, and I discovered a Vietnamese girl I had never seen before knew who I was and where I worked.

This all came about, when she called me a motherfucker in Vietnamese when I asked her to do my haircut over. I told her, "I really don't appreciate being called a motherfucker." She was amazed that I understood some Vietnamese, and that is when she spotted the name tag on my fatigues and instantly started apologizing. She knew I was in charge of the CMO for the 191st and probably thought I could get her fired. If she knew, then the cadre knew—hell, they probably knew our bunk assignments. There may not have been spies among us per se, but information could have been extorted from any number of people and for any number of reasons.

****

In the course of my work at the CMO and our daily trips across the bay, I had made friends with a Vietnamese shopkeeper. One day, after dropping off our cargo of Vietnamese workers, I strolled over to say hello. While I was standing there, he offered me some refreshments, some kind of unidentifiable substance in a Bireley's Orange bottle. I don't remember what the stuff was supposed to be, only that it was white and tasted terrible, and had the consistency of syrup. But to be nice, I drank the stuff and smiled all the time, as he grinned and nodded his head. I always wondered exactly what that stuff was. It didn't make me sick, which is more that I can say about other stuff I have ingested, like alcohol, and that tasted good.

When we were across the bay taking the Vietnamese home, we would often get something to drink from the marketplace vendors, and the drink of choice was lemonade. It was not the drink but the presentation that was unusual. They did not have cups or glasses to serve it in, so they used plastic bags. To drink the lemonade, you would bite a small hole in a corner of the bag, after the open end had been rubber banded shut, and suck the lemonade out. Of course, we GIs thought it was like having a breast in our hands and sucking on it, so we got refreshed and titillated at the same time.

While hunting for the lemonade vendor during our daily jaunts, I would wander around the local village market. There were all kinds of goods for sale at the stalls, which were set up kind of like a flea market in the States. Stolen cigarettes were sold there, as were clothes, hats, and many types of food—including snails.

The first time I wandered around the market, I was taken aback when I realized that what I had thought was black rope was actually flies. There were so many of them it looked like the awnings were held up with a black cord of some type, when it was really light-colored binder twine.

One woman had nothing but fish heads and guts for sale. Was that all she could afford to sell, or were fish guts a must-have, or maybe an impulse item? She had a large pile, about two feet high. I guess all the flies were extra. Although I never saw any customers, there must have been some demand for her goods or she would not have been there.

***

After I arrived at my permanent duty station, we attended a lecture from the chaplain concerning the Vietnamese. The lecture included an old, tired refrain about the dangers of having sex with whores and all the nasty things that could happen then and in the future, as well as a warning about the dangers of eating Vietnamese food in restaurants. What is really funny is that most of us, myself included, completely ignored the advice about the women, while refusing to eat any Vietnamese food from any source. If you can figure that one out, let me know.

Every once in a while, one of the better-looking whores would convince one of the NCOs—usually an E-5—to let her stay in his room overnight. This was strictly against policy, and the punishment could be harsh. But they would do it, and then some of them would try to drum up business for the girl. I don't think they looked upon it as pimping, but that's what it was. I bet the married NCOs didn't tell their wives about it in their letters home. Just another one of the interesting tidbits about life in Cam Ranh Bay that some men would just as soon forget.

BOYSANS

The Vill on main post Can Ranh Bay was always off-limits while I was stationed there, but I heard a lot about it from some old-timers. This was a different village than the one I spent a lot of time in, the village right in the middle of the base. The Vill was guarded by MPs and had the highest stack of concertina wire I have ever seen fencing it in; it must have been at least six coils high, if not more. But people still got out, including *boysans*, young boys of about seven to ten years of age who would generally make pests of themselves by trying to shine shoes, sell dirty pictures, and steal whatever was not tied down.

Once a *boysan* was trying to shine the boots of a truck driver who had spilled diesel fuel on his boots. Now, once diesel fuel is on a boot, it will never shine, no matter what is done to it. That *boysan* worked his butt off on those boots and they would not shine, and then the truck driver refused to pay him because of it. We all stood there and laughed at the kid, while the driver walked away—of course he had known when the kid started that the boots would never shine. Sounds pretty cruel, and it really was, but we were young and dumb enough to think it was pretty funny.

****

First sergeant for the 174th was Sergeant First Class (SFC) Frank Fisher. He was a pretty tough nut—hard core, as we used to call him. He was tough but fair, and I personally never had any problems with him, but some people did, and he was disliked by some men. A smoke grenade was thrown into his room once, just as a warning; it was meant to show him how easy it would have been to frag him with a real grenade.

Someone, I never found out who, taught a couple of the *boysans* to say, "Sergeant Fisher is a motherfucker." So, one night when SFC Fisher left the shower room, the *boysans* started chanting that, and since SFC Fisher had had a few too many beers, he could not hope to catch them. They kept it up for awhile, and SFC Fisher finally went to his room to get away from them. We all laughed until we cried. The sight of a drunken forty year old trying to catch a couple of eight olds makes me chuckle even to this day.

****

One morning, I was up pretty early. Walking out of the barracks, headed for the piss tubes, I came across several *boysans* asleep on the sand right front of the barracks—shows you how warm it was at night over there. Apparently they had been doing a little stealing during the night, because there between them was a case of C-Rations. To turn the tables on them, I took the C-rations from them, and put them in my wall locker.

Not too long afterward, everyone got up and the *boysans* woke to find their goods gone. Ooh, were those kids pissed. I don't know what they were saying, but I am sure it was bad. Since my bunk was pretty close to the door of the barracks and I was always up early, I know they were pretty sure I took their ill-gotten gains, but I said the hell with them, and we had ourselves a little midnight snack for a few days, at least on the rations that were edible.

DRAFT DODGER

As NCOIC (Non Commissioned Officer In Charge) of the CMO, it was my job to make sure everyone got to their assigned duty area, to assign crews to any new assignments, and most important, make sure everyone got paid on payday. This was a lot of responsibility for a twenty-one-year-old spec four.

Since very few of the Vietnamese spoke more than a few words of English, we had to have interpreters. A number of them worked there, both male and female. One male interpreter who worked mainly in the brass yard looked to be in his mid-twenties, was always well dressed, and was quite well-spoken. I cannot remember his name, but I figured then and am completely convinced now that he was a Vietcong.

Since I worked with him often, I got to know him pretty well, so one day I asked him how it was that he had never gotten drafted. He showed me his ID card, which said he was thirteen. Astonished, I asked "How can this be true?"

He said, "It was easy—I just gave the local official who was in charge of issuing ID cards thirty dollars." He was probably a senior cadre or something along that line; he was much too articulate for a run-of-the-mill VC. That is why he was able to bribe the local officials—the money, plus a veiled threat that the official and his family would end up dead or missing. Since not even the Vietnamese drafted thirteen year olds, he was safe. Some country, I thought.

One person working for the battalion did get drafted. He worked in the motor pool for the 606th Ordnance Company; his specialty was fixing flats. Most Army truck tires were held onto their rims with large rings called split rims, and they were a complete pain to remove. But this guy, whose nickname was Rat, could pop those split rims off in a heartbeat—he really had the knack.

Well, one day Rat came to see me and said he had been drafted and would be leaving. This caused a great amount of laughter and head-scratching among the GIs. We had a great time trying to describe the physical they had given him to qualify him for the draft, seeing how they failed to notice that he only had one eye. We laughed ourselves silly over that somewhat incredible oversight. But being the good citizen he was, he reported for the draft, and of course about two weeks later he came back (after someone finally noticed his one eye) and went back to work fixing flats in the 606th Motor Pool.

Not too long after Rat came back to work, I performed the only antiwar action of my entire life. I received a letter from headquarters, probably out of Long Binh or Bien Hoa, instructing me to send them the names of people I thought were dodging the draft. I sure as hell had one name I could give them, but at the same time I was furious. How dare they try to use me as a draft board when the place was so corrupt that a twenty-something could get an ID card saying he was thirteen? I didn't think it was my job to be an extension of the Vietnamese draft. Yes, I thought of my friends who had died for that place, and I knew he should do his part. But I thought it was just wrong what they wanted me to do, so I signed the form, dated it, and returned it with no names. The right thing to do? I hope so.

DO THEY HAVE IT?
Nameless bar, Nha Trang, 1969

Rock and roll blared over speakers, cigarette smoke was held in dense clouds by the ever-present humidity, and languid bargirls sprawled in the booths, waiting for the next customer. They had already pestered Elmquist and me, but we weren't interested on this day. Smoke from burning incense at a Buddhist shrine added to the almost liquid air. The conversation was muted by the music, but we could hear the B-girls speaking Vietnamese (probably calling us "number ten cheap charlies"). My buddy Elmquist and I were having a beer and a smoke, glad to be off duty for an entire day.

Pushing his hat back from his forehead and lighting up a smoke, Elmquist had just asked me something when my attention was suddenly diverted by the couple of Air Force guys in the bar, doing the same thing we were. One of them was saying to the Vietnamese bartender, "Saigon Tea doesn't having any booze in it." Saigon Tea was what the bargirls were always trying to get us to spend our money on.

The bartender was very attractive, with typical long black hair down to her waist. I think the Air Force GI was really just flirting with her, probably trying to get her into the sack. The bartender said it did have alcohol in it, and slammed a bottle of Seagrams down on the bar to prove it. She was just playing around, I think, giving as good as she got. But he did not believe her and kept teasing her about it.

Meanwhile, the other Air Force type was saying that the one thing he hated about Vietnamese women was that they didn't have any pubic hair. The why of this was never divulged to us. Again, I think he was saying this just to give the bartender a bad time, whether or not he actually cared was doubtful. But the bartender argued that they did.

The two of us, having had far too many beers, were listening to the conversation, which even in our state seemed really strange. We looked at each other between swallows of beer, with puzzled expressions on our faces.

Suddenly, the bartender stepped out from behind the bar. Saying, "I will prove that Vietnamese women have pubic hair." She pulled her pants down to her knees. We all nodded in agreement that indeed she did have hair down there. Then she pulled her pants up and gave us a look like she had just defended the honor of women everywhere, and went back behind the bar.

We joined into laughing and joking with the Air Force guys and had another beer and a smoke, and tried to figure out what we have just witnessed.

After a while, we left the bar and headed back to where the trucks were parked. In front of the bar, Elmquist was cussing a streak about something—since he was drunk, he was pretty loud. This attracted the attention of some lieutenant, who came up to us and asked

Elmquist to quiet down. He said, "There are a lot of nice people around, and they don't want to hear you swear."

Nice people!? All I saw were GIs and whores; the former didn't care, and the latter didn't understand. But since he was an officer, we said, "Yes, Sir," and went on our way. Where in the hell did he think he was, back home or something? We laughed our butts off after we got around the corner—and for sure, kept an eye open for any of those good people he spoke so highly of as we made our way back to get our weapons, climbed aboard the truck, and got ready for the ride back to Cam Ranh Bay.

****

Driving on Highway 1 to and from Nha Trang was always interesting and actually quite beautiful: *boysans* herded flocks of ducks in the rice paddies, farmers plowed the paddies behind water buffalo up to their knees in muck, small villages sat out in the distance, young women in brightly colored flowing ao dais appeared to float as they strolled along the pathways—an idyllic and bucolic scene if I had ever seen one. As long as you ignored the craters left by exploding mortar rounds along the side of the road, the scenery was great.

NHA TRANG

Every once in a while, the powers that be would decide to do something for us. Since we normally worked seven days a week, ten to twelve hours a day, with alerts thrown in at night, we needed some way to unwind, so we would get a one-day trip to Nha Trang, which was about thirty miles north of Cam Ranh Bay. Since we went through enemy country on the way, we carried weapons, steel pots, and a basic load of ammunition.

When we got to Nha Trang, we would turn in our weapons, because they weren't allowed in town—no one wanted a bunch of heavily armed drunks roaming around. The place where we turned in our weapons had flush toilets. It was the only place in Vietnam I ever saw such a thing. It was a novelty to flush.

They turned us loose and told us to be back in a couple of hours. The hours would be a beer-soaked blur of bargirls, Saigon Tea, dirt streets, and drunken GIs. The two times I went there, we always went to the same bar—I cannot remember the name. We would sit there and smoke cigarettes, drink beer, listen to music, and let the bargirls cage Saigon Tea out of us.

Those women could make a guy feel so special, like they had known him forever. It was amazing, though the fact that we were starved for any kind of attention from someone who was not male could have played a small part, I think. Those girls really knew how to make you feel good. They weren't whores, although for the right price, they probably would sleep with someone if they liked him enough. But it was fun to let them make you feel like they really felt something for you.

The last time I was in Nha Trang at that bar, we were sitting there, having a beer and a good time BSing with each other. I saw this young girl that looked to be about twelve years old come in from the back room and start going around the bar, stopping and standing in front of each GI.

When my turn came, and she stood in front of me, I realized she was deaf-mute. At first I could not figure what she wanted—and then it suddenly hit me. Using hand gestures, she was asking me if I wanted her to perform oral sex on me. For a moment, I became the deaf-mute, and then, recovering myself, I shook my head and she moved on to the next person. I thought, *Christ! Is this what we are doing here with all of our money, making whores out of children?* The sad thing is that I am sure she found plenty of takers among the throng at the bar. The picture of that girl standing in front of me is one of my most powerful and poignant memories of Vietnam; it haunts me to this day.

One thing about children in Nha Trang: they could not be trusted. When we walked around town, groups of *boysans* would approach us and act friendly. This was just a ruse to get close, because all of a sudden, they would be patting all your pockets, trying to figure out where your wallet and other valuables were. There would be six or eight of them doing this, so it behooved a GI to keep his wallet in his fatigues' front pocket or it would be gone in a flash.

Unfortunately, the only way to get rid them was to get mad and threaten to hit them. The threat actually had to be carried out now and again. I didn't have to injure them, but I did have to whack them hard enough that they knew I meant business. Then they would leave and go on to the next unsuspecting mark.

Boys were not the only scam artists around; little girls get an honorable mention, too. A friend of mine spotted a little girl sitting in the dust and crying her eyes out. Thinking she needed some money, he opened his wallet to give her a couple of bucks. Quick as a flash, she reached over, grabbed a twenty, and was gone before he knew what had happened. Trust in Vietnam was something to be doled out in very small doses.

REFUGEE CAMP

The road to the refugee camp was south of Cam Ranh, off Highway 1. It ran through some scrub jungle that came up right next to the road. Every so often, there would be some Koreans in full combat gear along the road, and they would wave to us as we passed by. Everyone was tense and halfway expecting an ambush. I can see the headlines now: "Entire ordnance detachment killed taking gifts to Vietnamese refugee camp."

One day, we were headed for the refugee camp to drop off some transistor radios. These had somehow been misdirected to our brass yard. Somewhere up the chain of command, the decision had been made to give them to the locals instead of sending them on to their correct destination. Just how the 174th Ordnance Detachment got delivery duty, I don't know, but there we were.

These radios had a crank on them to wind up a spring that generated power, since there were no batteries available to the refugees. I'm not sure what they would have listened to, but maybe AFVN (Armed Forces Vietnam), the radio station.

The camp was hacked out of the jungle at the base of the mountains surrounding Cam Ranh Bay. The road ended at the clearing that was the camp. Everyone seemed glad to see us, probably glad for the company. Since the camp was out in the sticks, I'm sure the people did not get to town very often. It was never made clear to us just where exactly these people were from or why they had become refugees.

We spent the day there with the people and made the best of it, giving away the radios and other gifts, and then headed back to Cam Ranh before it got dark. I'll bet the local VC had most of those radios within forty-eight hours of our visit, but hopefully the refugees got to enjoy them for a few hours.

SNAIL EATERS

All the Vietnamese who worked for the battalion except the KPs came across the bay and were dropped off at my office at the CMO every morning. It might take a while to get everyone assigned to their respective work areas, and, like I said, I might want to loan some of them out for the day. So while they were waiting for their assignments and rides, a lot of them would eat snails, like people in the States eat sunflower seeds.

These were small snails, with shells about one inch long and pointed at one end. It seemed everyone had their plastic bag of snails. I am not sure if they were cooked or eaten raw, having never tried them. The area out in front of my office was literally six inches deep in snail shells, some of them so old the sun had bleached them white. I once tried to get a group of the workers to clean up the shells, and they all looked at me like I was nuts, so I just put up with the shells and the snail eaters.

It was interesting to watch them eat their snacks. Some of them would pry the snail meat out of the shells with safety pins, which they kept conveniently pinned to the collars of their blouses. The other half were a little more direct in their pursuit of the local escargot. They just broke the pointed end of the snail shell with their front teeth and sucked out the contents. So we had safety-pin using and shell-breaking snail eaters. What was odd, at least from my point of view, was that safety-pin folks never became shell-breakers, nor did shell-breakers ever become safety-pin folks. In a contest between the betel nut ladies and the escargot eaters, I would go with the latter. I'll take empty shells over red spit anytime.

Seven

Across the Bay

ROADKILL, VIETNAM STYLE

We were heading south on Highway 1, taking the Vietnamese workers home at the end of another day. A long convoy of Vietnamese Army five-ton tractor trailer trucks loaded with 105 mm howitzer ammo passed us, headed north. There must have been fifteen or twenty of them. After we passed them, we came upon a dead Vietnamese man lying in the middle of the road. It may seem repugnant, but my reaction was no reaction at seeing the dead guy—he was just another pothole in the road to be avoided. Around his head there was a large pool of blood, and off the side of road lay his motorcycle. His long hair was slowly soaking up his blood.

Someone next to me asked, "You think he's dead?"

I said, "What do you think, genius?"

The dead guy looked to be in his mid-twenties. Since almost everyone in Vietnam over the age of eighteen was in the military, we figured the dead guy must have been a draft dodger, because he sure wasn't in the service with that long hair.

Since I didn't actually see what happened, I imagined that the dead guy was headed north, just like the convoy of five-ton trucks. I pictured him weaving in and out of the column of trucks, with his long hair flying the wind, when one of the truck drivers decided to exact a little revenge. All it took was a little tap, and down he went, and the deed was done. No one even had to slow down or disrupt the column.

We passed by, as did everyone else. No one was stopping, just driving around and going on their way like everyone would do in the States, as if it were a dog or deer lying dead in the road. We guessed the MPs or Vietnamese police would drop by and do something sooner or later. When we came back, heading back to Cam Ranh Bay, the dead guy was gone; only the stain remained.

It may seem odd that we didn't stop, but we weren't allowed to stop anywhere except at designated areas, and since there were no telephones around, there was nothing we could have done. But also that was just the way it was there: no one got worked up about a dead Vietnamese man.

HIGHWAY 1, OR THE DAY IT RAINED WHITE MICE

In what seemed like slow motion, I watched the Army issue Dodge pickup truck come around the curve on Highway 1, heading north. On my right, a jeep full of "white mice" was backing up to where I stood. I could see what was going to happen, and there was absolutely nothing I could do to prevent it.

It was a scene out of a bad movie. The Dodge was going maybe fifty miles per hour and the jeep was in reverse; the two vehicles hit with explosive force. It was like they hit a mine. The Vietnamese police were blasted into the air like leaves in the wind. There must have been six of them flying through the air—and then there was silence before the bodies thudded to earth. The only way I ever saw the police travel was in these ragtop jeeps with as many as they could cram inside. The two GIs sat there in the smashed truck, in shock. And what was I doing there in my front row seat, you might ask?

It all began earlier that day at our work area, when Sergeant Keenan had asked me if I wanted to stop at the whorehouse we passed each day when we took the Vietnamese home. It was risky, because we weren't allowed off the truck, and if we were caught it was an automatic demotion in rank and dock in pay. But I decided, *What the heck, what are they gonna do, send me to Vietnam?* (Well, they could have transferred me to the infantry, I suppose...) So I said, "Yeah, I'll go."

My detachment was responsible for taking about fifty Vietnamese workers home each day from the brass yard. At the end of each day we would load them up in a five-ton tractor trailer, and across the bay we would go. Our destination that day was between two small towns. After dropping us off, the truck would go to the next town, drop off the workers, and pick us up on the way back.

After we were done, but before the truck came to pick us up, just moments before the white mice died in front of me, something happened. I was sitting in the entrance to the interior patio of the house, waiting, and looked up in time to see a Vietnamese man enter. He had been riding a Honda 50 motorcycle. Otherwise all in black, he wore a GI-issue bush hat and had a .45 automatic pistol strapped to his hip. He paid no attention to me, but I know he saw me. He continued out of sight into the back.

As far as I knew, there were no regional forces in the area, and he wasn't in the Vietnamese army dressed like that. So the question is, was he a Vietcong? I have always thought he must have been, but I don't know for sure. Since I did not have a weapon and he did, there wasn't much I could do anyway—and even if I'd had one, I doubt I would have done anything. I guess he was there for the same reason the two of us were.

It dawned on me later what a dangerous stunt we had pulled. We could have disappeared without a trace, never to be seen alive again. I can just see the telegram my mother would have received: that her son was missing from a whorehouse and was now an MIA, with *missing* being the operative word, not the action. Oh yeah, she would have loved that. But I didn't have time to consider this before the crash.

The reason the white mice stopped in the first place was the way the girl standing out front was dressed. The curious thing about the area was that prostitution was OK if a girl was wearing shorts, but not OK if the girl was wearing a minidress. The difference is lost in translation. And, of course, the girl on the shoulder of the road advertising her wares was wearing a minidress instead of shorts when the police passed by. Instead of turning around, they started backing up—and that's when the two GIs in their Dodge pickup truck came along.

So there I was. Standing where I did not belong, terrified I'd be caught, and standing in a place where the real police, the MPs, would soon show up. Maybe the god in charge of fools was watching out for me that day. If so, he was a little hard on the Vietnamese police in his zeal to protect me from myself.

Did I check the injured and dead and apply first aid? No. I just wanted to get out of there before the MPs arrived. I saw the truck coming and I knew I was saved. The truck wove its way through the carnage; we ran across the road, jumped on board, shouted, "Let's go!" and left the scene behind us. Who died, who was crippled for life, I never knew, and for years did not care. Now I wish I had at least checked on the GIs, but I did not.

PARATROOPS

Across Cam Ranh Bay from main post, Khanh Hoa Province, 1969,

On our way back from dropping off the Vietnamese workers, we heard airplanes overhead—generally nothing unusual, since we were across the bay from the Air Force base, but these were different. Looking up, we saw a couple of Vietnamese C-119 flying boxcars right overhead; almost immediately, parachutes blossomed out behind them. Since none of us had ever seen paratroops before, we slowed down for a look. They looked like they were going to land about a mile from us.

It must have been a practice drop, since we were in a pretty secure area, at least secure in the day. When one of the last paratroopers jumped out of the plane and opened his parachute, something came loose and he started falling. Someone said, "Hey, look at that!" and someone else mused, "Wonder what that is?" Keeping our eyes on the falling object, we all wondered out loud what was happening. It soon became apparent that it was one of the paratrooper's boots that was clearly visible as it fell.

How this happened, I do not know—maybe he forgot to tie his boot tight enough. All I know is that it caused many comments about the quality of Vietnamese paratroopers. Most GIs had a poor opinion of Vietnamese troops in general, and this scene served to reinforce our thinking. We wondered what kind of walk back to the pickup point he was going to have with only one boot. I suspect it was not fun. We left, and went back to base, leaving the paratroopers alone.

There is an old saying in the Army: "Only bird shit and idiots fall from the sky." On this particular day, there was at least one idiot, and I bet his fellow paratroopers never let him forget it. But one last comment: the landing must have been a bitch.

AND WHAT WAS I DOING THERE?

Eight

Wildlife

ANIMALS AND BIRDS

I have already mentioned the cockroaches and rats that abounded in the barracks, but other critters lived nearby, too. Some kind of small lizards lived right along with us, perhaps some kind of gecko. They used to come out at night and run around, and they chirped just like birds, reminding me of the English sparrows back home. Other than waking me up once in a while, though, they weren't really pests.

Out in the storage areas, there were a number of really large lizards; I remember one in particular, which had black and white stripes on its tail. And one time, down at the renovation line, we caught what seemed like some kind of monitor lizard. It was about four feet long. It had apparently gotten into something, maybe the acetone we had been using to remove paint nearby, which later killed it.

The storage areas were also home to perhaps the most iconic symbol of Vietnam (at least for Vietnam vets), and that was the "fuck you lizard." I never saw one, but I suffered through many barrages of their insults on guard duty. It went sort of like this: "Fuck you, fuck you, fuck you too," for the whole night. After a while, you almost did begin to take it personally. It was like some demented Vietnamese guy was out in the brush, screaming insults at you all night.

These lizards' existence has been used as a filter to screen out "wannabe Vietnam vets," because if you don't know what a fuck you lizard is, you weren't there. I myself have been tested this way.

Other than a few terns, I saw very few birds at Cam Ranh Bay. A few English sparrows actually did show up around the barracks, but it must have been too hot for them to nest successfully. All the time I was there, I only saw a couple of them.

One time, a large green sea turtle dragged itself out of the South China Sea, came up the beach right behind the break shack at the renovation line, and laid eggs. This was really interesting to watch, and I'm glad it did not trod on one of the mines that were rumored to be planted on the beach. We checked on her progress each time we took a break, and everyone took an interest in the egg-laying. What was kind of weird was that no one bothered her—it was more like we all protected her. Those young turtles had more mothers than they ever suspected.

One night, while walking around the company area on CQ, I heard a strange noise. Figuring it was a rat, I directed the light from my flashlight toward it, and saw a strange animal there. It looked like it had scales all over its body, including the tail. I had never seen anything like it, and had no idea what it was. Years later, while watching a show on PBS, I finally identified the animal. It was a pangolin, a kind of anteater.

SNAKES

"MAAAAACCCC!!!!" Someone was screaming my overseas nickname; actually, he was more shrieking it. I was working in the CMO.

My small office was in the same building as the battalion's commo shack, and that's where the scream was coming from. I could tell that something was really wrong, so I ran over there as fast as I could.

The staff sergeant who was in charge of the area stood there clutching his chest, breathing so hard that I thought he was having a heart attack or had seen a ghost. I asked, "What's wrong?" and he just pointed to the floor. I looked where he was pointing, and there was a snake—a cobra, to be precise. Not a very big one, but a cobra nonetheless. With its neck hood spread out, and hissing like a teakettle. Without further discussion, we worked together, using a broom to push the snake into a cardboard box.

After I finally got the staff sergeant calmed down, he explained what had happened. He had decided that the commo shack needed a good cleaning, so he grabbed a broom and got to work. Behind one of the work benches, he spotted what he thought was a piece of electrical tape on the floor—not an uncommon thing in a commo shack. Reaching back behind the bench, he grabbed it, planning to throw it away. And that, of course, is when I heard my name being screamed. About two feet long and approximately three quarters of an inch across, the snake was black as coal. It really did look exactly like a piece of electrical tape.

I finally got the staff sergeant calmed down, after about twenty minutes or so. I think he really was about to have a heart attack. Then we decided to take a look at our captive in the box. But that snake was stone-cold dead. I can't figure out what killed it, because we just swept into the box with a broom, and didn't crush it or anything. Maybe the shock of seeing the staff sergeant was too much for the poor thing.

I was used to seeing snakes in Vietnam; they were common in the ammunition storage areas. I remember one really big cobra that was something like ten or twelve feet long. Someone had killed it in Yankee Area, I believe. When working at our renovation, we were always finding snakes in the ammunition boxes that had been there a while.

The snakes in the ammo boxes were small, about a foot and a half long, and kind of light green in color. Assuming all snakes were poisonous, we killed them. We called these ones "two steppers," since we heard that, if bitten, you would take two steps before dying. For all I know, they were actually Vietnamese garter snakes and posed no threat. But nobody knew or had any way of finding out, so they were all killed.

Nine

Ambush Patrol

"MAYBE WE'RE TOO CLOSE"

As I jumped down from the deuce-and-a-half, someone called, "Hey Mac, seen the bulletin board?" All duty rosters were posted and had to be read at least twice a day. I went over and there was my name, McCormick, William—Ambush Patrol, along with the names of eight other men in the detachment. I thought, *Good grief, someone has thought up another way to try and kill me.* We were to meet in front of the orderly room in about an hour. I went to my bunk, had a smoke, and got my gear together.

In an hour we all met Lieutenant Crites, who was wearing a .45 pistol, web gear, and a bush hat. He certainly looked the part. He waited while everyone drew their weapons. The lieutenant told me to forget my rifle, since I would be carrying the M79 grenade launcher. Then, giving me the PRC 25, which we called the "prick twenty-five," he said I would be RTO (Radio Man) for the patrol. Someone called out, "Hey, Mac, you know they shoot the radioman first!" and I thought, Oh great!

The lieutenant said we had better have a commo check to see if the radio worked and the battery was any good. We stood about ten feet apart, and I could hear him, but he could not hear me. Shrugging, he said, "We're probably too close—I'm sure it works fine."

TOO CLOSE? I thought that was really stupid, and couldn't be right, but he was an officer and I was just a spec four, so I said, "OK," and kept my mouth shut. That was really stupid of me, since our lives could have depended on that radio working as it was supposed to.

As we boarded the truck, each of us received two hand grenades. I thought, *This is getting way too serious for an ordnance guy*. The CO said if overrun, we were to throw one grenade and make our way back to the wire. I didn't ask what we were supposed to do with the other one.

Off we went to Yankee Ammunition Storage Area. Dismounting at the guard bunker, we went through the wire, down into a ravine, and up a road of sorts. About three quarters of the way there, alongside a large brush-covered dune, the lieutenant said, "This is a good spot." He positioned everyone on both sides of the road so we would not shoot each other—at least he said he hoped not. We were so exposed that I couldn't see any VC or NVA walking into our ambush; even a blind man wouldn't have stumbled into us. The CO told me to call in and report our position—and of course the radio did not work. Some captain inside the wire must have finally figured out what was wrong, and the rest of the night we communicated with him by pressing the talk button, once for yes and twice for no.

The captain asked if we wanted some flares for illumination. The lieutenant said yes, so I keyed the talk bar once, and night turned to day.

Now, the 81 mm mortar is a very powerful weapon, and the flares go off about two hundred feet in the air. The problem began when the flares deployed above us. Once the parachute opened for the flare, the bottom part would fall to the ground. Made of steel, it weighed approximately one pound.

After the flares went off, the bases started falling to earth with a whooshing sound, crashing down through the brush, and landing with loud thuds. It was like being under attack. Since we had set up out in the open and weren't wearing our steel pots, we stood a good chance of being hit. We were terrified, but the lieutenant was as calm as could be.

As the bases continued to rain down and scare of daylights out of all of us except him, I started thinking that, if I had to give up my life for my country, I was hoping it would be for something more heroic than being hit in the head by the butt end of a flare. Finally, after a near miss, the lieutenant asked to have the flares stopped, and I frantically keyed the radio and got the bombardment stopped.

Later on, he got the idea that the radio just needed an antenna. He found some commo wire and had me tie it to a tree about twenty feet away, but of course this made no difference; the radio still did not work.

The sky slowly started to lighten; daylight was not far away, and the patrol was almost over. We had seen no Vietcong or NVA, blind or otherwise—a good thing, because we probably would have all been killed or really had to use those two grenades we had been given. We made our way back to where the truck would pick us up with a slightly better understanding of what the infantry went through on a daily basis. Hopefully, they were a lot better at it than we were.

AND WHAT WAS I DOING THERE?

Ten

Entertainment

IT BEGAN TO LOOK LIKE A RIOT

I noticed the nurse when she first entered the stage area, and I commented on her looks to the GI on my left. She had only taken a few steps when she suddenly staggered and then slowly sagged to the ground. Seconds earlier, a beer can, probably filled with sand, arced over my head, and I had enough time to think, *That thing is bound to hit someone.* People rushed to her aid and carried her out of the area. I still remember the anguished look on her escort's face as he scanned the crowd, looking for the can thrower, and no doubt swearing at all of us.

Welcome to *The Bob Hope Show*, Cam Ranh Bay, 1968. I had a feeling Mom and Dad were not going to see any of this on their TV set back home.

When we heard Bob Hope was coming, we were as excited as school kids. We knew he was coming, but not where or when until the exact day. When the day finally arrived, we all piled into a truck and took off to see the show.

When we arrived, we were directed to sit behind a taped-off area, and we were kind of disappointed to be so far from the stage. But I told myself, *That's all right—I can still see, and it is* The Bob Hope Show. What more could any GI want for Christmas, except maybe an earlier DEROS? Pretty soon we observed the reason for the taped-off area when they brought in wounded men from the hospital, the 6th CC. We figured that was OK, they had paid their price for a better seat. When officers began to fill in the area around the stage is when the trouble really started. Wounded men were one thing, but perfectly healthy officers were something else altogether. That was when the barrage of beer cans started, fueled by too much beer and dislike for officers in general. It was beginning to look more like a riot than *The Bob Hope Show.* A squad of heavily armed MPs worked their way through the crowd, looking for troublemakers, and things quieted down quite a bit—no one wanted to get arrested.

After a while, directly in front of me, a man in hospital blue pajamas got up and began chanting, "First Cav. number one! First Cav. number one!" Exactly why he did this bit of cheerleading for the First Cavalry Division was a mystery; maybe he thought we rear area troops needed to know.

Someone took offense, and he became another beer can casualty. When the can hit his head, it made a strange hollow bonk, and he hit the ground. Everyone laughed: no more cheerleading, no more Mr. First Cav. No one came to his aid; nurses were one thing, but goofball GIs were another. Even the other wounded laughed at him. He found it best to keep his thoughts to himself after that.

Sometime after Mr. First Cav. had been dealt with, a couple of men came out on the stage with movie cameras, wanting everyone to wave and shout for them, which everyone did with enthusiasm. If anyone saw that episode of *The Bob Hope Show*, they may remember those scenes of all the happy waving GIs. However, they could not have done that later and gotten the same results.

Soon after the filming of the happy GIs, some workmen began

building a scaffolding right in front of the stage. We all watched wondering, *What the hell is going on?* But we soon found out. What was being built was a platform for all the cameras, so the show could be filmed for the folks back home. By the time it was finished, we could not see a blasted thing, and we all started wondering who this whole show was for: us, or the folks back home? General consensus was that we were just props, and the show was actually meant for a stateside audience. They sure as hell had better seats than we did. So there we were, right where we had wanted to be, and it turned out we were in the wrong place. At that point, happy, waving GIs we were not.

When Bob Hope came out on stage and started making jokes about being sandblasted in the shower, though, everyone started laughing and things settled down some. We still could not see much, but at least we could hear, and that was better than nothing. I don't remember much about any of the other acts, but do remember laughing at the gags and trying to see who was on stage.

The last act has always stayed with me, however, and that was the Golddiggers. The last song was "Silent Night," and just as the Golddiggers started to sing, it began to rain. Now, anyone who has been in Southeast Asia knows how it can rain. No thunder and lightning, no sprinkle-dinkle, no preliminaries or anything like that—just a solid wall of water that comes crashing down. But those ladies hung in there and sang their hearts out for us in the pouring rain. I think there were a lot of throats with lumps in them then; there was one in mine. If it had not been raining so hard, it might have been hard to find a dry eye. Everyone around me stayed to the end in the downpour and got soaking wet, but that was a moment to savor, a once in a lifetime experience, I think.

Even after that, we were still pissed at not being able to see, even when Bob Hope noticed and tried to get people to move to the side—it didn't work; we were too far away. But thinking about it later, I see things differently: those people were there for us, risking their lives and their careers (such was the divisiveness of the Vietnam War). *The Bob Hope Show* gave me and a lot of other men some (mostly) pleasant memories in an otherwise miserable place and time. As I think back on it, so what if we could not see? We could hear, and as is the case for most things that are really important, it really was the thought that counted.

Eleven

Sick Call

EVERYONE WITH A SUSPECTED CASE

I woke up one morning with a really bad sore throat. I figured it was another case of strep throat, which I suffered from intermittently my whole time in the Army. After putting up with it for a day or so, I went on sick call. After morning formation, I walked over to the dispensary to see a medic. While waiting, I witnessed a very funny incident, and probably something that said a lot about GIs in general.

The dispensary was not open yet, so I waited outside with everyone else. There were at least fifty men waiting, maybe as many as sixty or seventy. One guy was playing the harmonica, and, amazingly, one guy there had gone to basic training with me. He was just down from the DMZ after serving as a medic on a Dustoff helicopter. The only thing he would say about that duty was, "It was really ugly." I did not inquire any further; it was apparent that it was not something he wanted to talk about.

After we sat in the blazing sun for a time, a medic came out of the building and hollered, "All right, listen up." What happened next makes me laugh to this day. The medic hollered, "All men here for smear tests or for suspected cases of clap should line up over to the left side of the dispensary." It was like a stampede to the left side of the building. In two minutes, only one other GI and I were left on the right side. Of all my memories of Vietnam, that moment is right up there with the best of them. Remembering how everyone got up and ran to the left still makes me chuckle and shake my head in wonder.

Guess that shows what a lot of GIs are doing with their off-duty time. I felt really self-conscious that I did not have the clap or some other sexually transmitted disease. On the flip side, I did get to see a doctor really quickly, since there was no line on my side.

The doctor decided I had a bacterial infection of the throat. How I got it was unknown—no, not that way. They gave me some penicillin pills to take and sent me on my way. Well, the pills did no good, and I was barely able to eat—and forget about smoking. My ration card was blank during the time I had that malady. After a couple of days, the pills were gone, but the pain was not, so I went back to the dispensary.

The doctor on duty looked at my throat, gave me a slip of paper and told me to go into another room. There, I gave the slip of paper to a Vietnamese nurse and she motioned to me to drop my pants and bend over. I thought, *What the heck is going on here?* Well, since the pills did not work, they decided to break out the heavy artillery, and give me a shot of penicillin.

Reaching into a small refrigerator, the nurse retrieved the biggest damn syringe I had ever seen—it was as big as a pint milk bottle—and screwed a needle into it. She threw that thing into my butt like she was playing darts. That syringe was ice-cold from being stored in a refrigerator, and it hurt like hell as she pushed the plunger.

I went back to duty, and within a couple of days, I was on the mend. Of course, no one believed me when I said I'd had a throat infection.

Everyone clapped every time I walked by, and all the truck drivers hit every bump in the road whenever I rode in a truck for a week, and I was forced to stand—sitting down was out of the question.

During that same memorable visit to the dispensary, another incident happened that was just as strange as the other was funny, making the whole morning very odd in deed. While walking down the hallway, I spotted an NCO from the company next to us, the 46th Ordinance. He was sitting there on a bench, looking like death warmed over. His face was literally grey. He had the look of someone dead who just hadn't yet found the right spot for lying down. I had never seen anyone look quite like that. Actually, the only person I ever saw who looked like that really was dead.

Later on that evening, we had a formation, and I asked our CO if he knew what had happened to that guy. Well, it seems that the day before he had been up to Nha Trang, out drinking with an NCO from my detachment, Staff Sergeant Shannon. While in some bar, he had been giving the female bartender a lot of crap. This was believable, because he really wasn't a very nice person. I didn't care for him either as a person or as an NCO.

Anyway, the rumor was that she spiked his 33 (a Vietnamese beer, also known as Ba Muoi Ba) with ground glass. This would have been easy to do, since 33 was normally served warm, and thus you'd put ice in your glass, like you would a glass of iced tea. Nothing happened to Shannon, who was sitting right next to him, but who did not harass the bartender. I don't know if he survived. As far as I know, he never came back from the dispensary and was never seen again.

Of course, that was not the only time I ever went to the dispensary. Heat rash was the millstone around my neck for an entire year. It started off as just an irritating rash, but soon morphed into open running sores, itching ulcers, like a good case of poison oak. I went to the doctor time after time, trying to get something to cure the affliction, but to no avail.

When I first arrived in Vietnam, I thought it really odd that many men did not wear underwear or T-shirts. I began to understand after my battle with heat rash began. The problem is that the elastic band in underwear is the perfect breeding ground for whatever causes heat rash, and a person's crotch seems to be one of its favorite places. Armpits are another one, but my main problem area was below the belt, actually anywhere my skin was chafed by clothing. So I soon began going commando, to use a term from today. This brought some relief, but did not entirely rid me of my torment.

Finally, during another visit to the dispensary, they gave me a bottle of liquid to apply directly to the sores. Who knows what it was, but I suspect it was just alcohol with yellow dye in it. This stuff burned like there was no tomorrow. Since most of the sores were in my crotch, you can imagine the contortions I went through after an application. I'm sure my fellow GIs were more than a little amused at my nightly dance. The stuff did clear up the open sores, but did not stop others from starting, so it was a constant battle.

After struggling for months against this crotch-eating rash, a friend in the barracks suggested I use talcum powder. I managed to score a bottle and began using it, and lo and behold—that rash was gone within a week. As long as I used that powder, I never had a problem. My cure was suggested by a guy from the backwoods of Virginia, who may or may not have graduated from high school. Makes me wonder about those doctors and why they didn't think of it.

Twelve

Bad Decisions

YOU REALLY DO GET CRAZY

We were watching a movie in the company area when the shooting started. It sounded like a whole M-14 magazine was being emptied somewhere down the road. Shootings on main post Cam Ranh Bay weren't common, so everyone paid attention. Then we all looked at each other, waiting. No alert was called, so we figured it must have been between GIs—and unfortunately, we were right on the money.

It turned out that some men from a signal company had confronted a GI from the 33rd Ordnance Company, part of my battalion, who was apparently getting ready to go on guard duty. The signal company GIs accused the 33rd man of stealing a tape recorder. It turned out that he owned a similar one. After things were cleared up, everyone left and went back to their hooches. But that was not the end of the story, not by a long way.

The man from the 33rd solved his own problem by grabbing a magazine, walking out to the PSP (Perforated Steel Plate), kneeling down, and putting twenty rounds into the signal company's hooch.

Rumor was that he killed two and wounded eight, but I do not know if that is true. I do know that he got ten years in Leavenworth for his seemingly irrational act.

After a person had been in a place like Vietnam for a long enough time, acts like this started to seem like they made sense. I do not know why—maybe some kind of depression, because it seemed like your year would never end.

At one point, I found myself making plans with a certain friend to murder a member of our detachment. It made perfect sense to us at the time. Fortunately, we never had the chance to put our plan into action. Now I am amazed that we planned such a thing, and am really thankful that we could not carry out our plan. Boy, am I thankful. When people stop caring about themselves, it makes surviving that much more difficult

Is it rational to have irrational thoughts about killing perceived enemies in a combat zone, no matter who they are? All I know is that I would have had no problem killing that man. Is there a point of no return for rational thought?

REALLY DUMB THINGS

As I said, I kept my eye on the people around me in order to go home alive at the end of my year, but I guess I forgot to keep an eye on myself. I did some really dumb things during that year that obviously had nothing to do with rational thinking. One of these was the trip to the whorehouse—dumb, really dumb—which was right at the top of the list, but there were others.

"Hey Mac, give me a cigarette?" One of my sweat-soaked fellow sufferers asked, and I threw him the pack and lighter. This was your standard question in the service, except we were in an ammunition storage area. Leaning back against the cool steel projectiles on a pallet, I lit up and enjoyed my own smoke. Smoking among the ammo—dumb, you say? Yep, but we did it.

That particular day was exceptionally hot, and we had been working on a batch of eight-inch projectiles. When we took our break, the only shade was back in the pad of ammunition, a hundred feet long and sixty feet deep, and stacked probably four pallets high; we would lean up against the ammo that was still cool from the nighttime.

Of course, we weren't supposed to even have lighters in the storage areas. There was a place to put them at the entrance to the area, but we never did. We just put them in the blouses of our boots and no one was the wiser. It did all depend on who was in charge of the detail if we could get away with smoking. So there we were, smoking amid maybe two hundred tons of ammunition. Good thing U.S. ammo is really safe stuff, because one wrong move there and we would have been vaporized. But I don't remember that bothering us very much; I guess we had been there too long to care. There was the general sentiment: "This year will never end," and I guess I can't blame all stupid things on that, but it did make an impact.

Among my many jobs in Vietnam were assistant CBR NCO (Chemical Biological Radiation) and assistant armorer. One day, we received an order telling us we needed to change all the filters and gaskets in the company's gas masks. Even though we never used them, orders are orders, so we started the process of ordering the parts. The problem was, none of us knew how to order the parts, so the CO had a SFC help us out with the paper work. Wow! Some help he turned out to be.

For our small company, we needed about sixty filters and gaskets to switch everything out. About two weeks after our "expert" helped us, a dump truck pulled up to the company area with our load of filters and gaskets. The bed of the truck was filled with our replacement parts. I honestly cannot remember if it was sixteen thousand or sixty thousand, but it was how many they were able to fit in the back of a dump truck. Some help that SFC was—hell, we could have done that badly by ourselves. Christ, we had enough filters and gas mask gaskets for every troop in Cam Ranh Bay and then some. We took what we needed, and sent the rest back to the depot, cussing the SFC all the while.

Thirteen

Out of There

LEAVING

The wheels of the plane left the ground, and everyone started cheering, clapping, and shaking hands as Vietnam disappeared behind us. We were finally leaving, heading home. That was one of the best feelings I have ever felt. I survived. No one had managed to kill or maim me, no one from either side. I was sitting with my friend, Larry Poplin, from Kansas. We met on the plane going to Vietnam, served at Long Binh together, went to Cam Ranh on the same plane, and ended up in the same company for a year. Now we were flying home to the States together. I have always thought that was really something.

When it came time for me to go home, all I had thought about was leaving. I was unprepared for the pangs of regret that surged to the surface when the truck pulled out of the company area. All of a sudden, it dawned on me that I would never see these men again. I remembered several men I had forgotten to say good-bye to, and almost jumped off the truck to do it.

It wasn't like leaving a job. I was with these men twenty-four hours a day, seven days a week, and had made some real friends—and that was now disappearing right in front of me. I was startled by the thought. Some of these men I would have trusted with my life, and that would even be true today.

And so I came home, like thousands of other men. But I have always wondered about that part of me that I left in Vietnam. I tried for years to exorcise it, but failed. I've finally figured out that it is part of my personality now and I've accepted it. I did some things over there I am not particularly proud of, but I've put it down to another life.

I looked up my old CO, Vern Mello, a couple of years ago, and we are now the best of friends. In the course of our conversations, he said I should be proud of the work the 174th had done in Vietnam, and even though we didn't get into the fighting, our job was important and did save lives of men in the field. I have looked up a number of men I was stationed with. Some are happy and have stayed in touch, some are not happy and do not want to. But that's OK; I made the effort. The depressing discovery has been how many men are now permanently disabled from Agent Orange. Makes me wonder what lurks in my future...

HOME

Ah! Home, that mythical place we all came from, and longed to return to. The longer we served, the better it grew in our minds. The winters weren't as cold, the summers were never hot. Home just had to be better than where we were. Whether it actually was or not, was another question, but at least in most of our homes, no one was trying to kill us, and we could trust the people that lived around us.

As we changed, home was the constant that kept us focused on the goal: getting out of Vietnam and returning there. Whatever was there got people through the year: girlfriends, wives, jobs, cars, schools, parents. For me, for some reason it was a coat, of all things. I had worn that coat on many trips in the outdoors, so maybe it was my connection to something better. Of course there was also a woman I used to think about, but I never told her. She helped me a lot, although she does not know it. I suppose I should tell her one of these days, since I am back in contact with her. She was a connection to my other life, and she helped.

Home had become this Eden in my mind. And when I finally did get home, I found it, well, boring. After dreaming about home and what I would do there, I ended up leaving for my next duty station early, just to get away. It was so claustrophobic, I could not stand it. Rooms seemed so small I had to sleep with the door open, and forget about wearing pajamas. I knew I should love my parents' house and them, but I just had to leave.

I found normal conversation extremely difficult. I would sweat and stutter, and felt very uncomfortable trying to talk to even my closest friends. When I flew back to Fort Riley, Kansas, the stewardess that tried to talk to me must have thought I was an idiot. She was very pretty and friendly and sat down next to me, but I was so tongue-tied, she finally got up and left me to my own demons. With GIs, I was fine, but it took about six months before I was able to talk to other people without any problem. Of course, one of the problems was trying to have a regular conversation without swearing. In Vietnam, swearing was normal conversation. But swearing was not acceptable at home, at least not my home.

So it was a difficult transition, to say the least. I'm sure my parents felt the same, since the son they got back was not the same one who had left for Vietnam. The problem was that my parents never seemed to realize that I had changed, and expected me to be the same person I had been and to act the way I had before. My brother-in-law had tried to tell them what to expect—he was a Vietnam vet and knew what was coming—but they ignored his advice. Their inability to see me as another person caused problems that I never really overcame.

One last word on coming home: color had become shocking. Everything was green in Vietnam, including fatigues, boots, T-shirts, underwear, socks, handkerchiefs, hats, and trucks—and if it wasn't green, then it was black. It was amazing to see all the colors around me. It was almost to the point of being overwhelming and took some getting used to. That may sound insignificant to a lot of people, but unless you have experienced it, it is difficult to understand.

Epilogue

LOT'S WIFE, OR A STAR TREK MOMENT?

Ten years after getting out of the Army, I was working at a bookstore. Great job, good working conditions, terrible pay—but for a reader like me, it was heaven, and I loved working there. In those days, I had tried to put Vietnam down as a past life, and not think about it at all, if possible.

The store was in a suburban shopping mall, like hundreds of others around the country. Since I was the assistant manager, it was one of my jobs to open the store in the morning, so I usually got there pretty early.

On this particular day, I was walking across the deserted parking lot, heading toward the door to get started on my day. As I walked along, thinking of the workday ahead of me, I heard a helicopter over head—in itself no big thing, since there used to be several military bases close to town.

Out of habit, I looked up. All of a sudden, I was Lot's wife, but instead of a pillar of salt, I was a pillar of flesh, frozen in time, a monument built by my memory in a land of pavement and vehicles.

What I saw was a Cobra helicopter gunship. I had not seen a Cobra since I left Vietnam in 1969, and it caused me to have some kind of flashback. The sight of that helicopter stopped me dead in my tracks; I'm sure I was only in that state for a split second, but it seemed longer, much, much longer. I remember nothing of that time, except the helicopter as it crossed my field of vision. When I came to, or regained consciousness, or whatever it was, I wasn't sure where I was or where I had been.

I scrutinized the parking lot very carefully to make sure I was where I thought I was. Looking around that parking lot had to be one of the most peculiar sensations I have ever experienced. Not knowing where I was left me feeling very strange indeed. I stomped on the blacktop to make sure I really was there.

I finally decided that I really was on my way to work, not back in Vietnam, and went about my business of opening up the bookstore, physically none the worse for wear, despite my journey into the past. Talk about an out-of-body experience—we are talking major goose bumps. If it were not like being Lot's wife, it was like something out of Star Trek, when they would use the transporter beam to send people down to an alien planet's surface.

I have seen many helicopters since then, Cobras included, and that particular feeling has never happened again, thank goodness. I suppose it shows just how powerful a memory can be, when it can instantly transport a person back in time—and scare the crap out of them.

About the Author

 William "Bill" McCormick was born and raised in California, spending most of his childhood in Humboldt County and then Sacramento. He graduated high school in 1965, attended college for awhile and then joined the Army in October of 1967. He was sent to Vietnam in September of 1968 and spent his whole tour with the 174th Ord. Det. in Cam Ranh Bay. Upon leaving Vietnam in 1969 he was sent to Fort Riley, Kansas for a few months and was discharged as a SGT E-5 in 1970. Bill returned to college, earning a BA in U.S. History from California State University, Sacramento in 1976. A serious bicycle rider for over thirty years, he has worked as a bike mechanic and has cycled around the U.S. and Canada. After working for the State of California for twenty-one years, Bill retired in 2009. This is his first published book.

Made in the USA
Monee, IL
07 July 2026